T0209659

HEALING
EVER AFTER

KRISTIE ADDAIR GUARD

WESTBOW
PRESS®
A DIVISION OF THOMAS NELSON
& ZONDERVAN

WestBow Press books may be ordered through booksellers or by contacting:

WestBow Press
A Division of Thomas Nelson & Zondervan
1663 Liberty Drive
Bloomington, IN 47403
www.westbowpress.com
844-714-3454

ISBN: 979-8-3850-0087-6 (sc)
ISBN: 979-8-3850-0056-2 (hc)
ISBN: 979-8-3850-0057-9 (e)

Library of Congress Control Number: 2023911197

Print information available on the last page.

WestBow Press rev. date: 8/24/2023

CONTENTS

ACKNOWLEDGMENTS

Katelyn, Kelsey, and Brooke, this book is dedicated to you. You have been my guiding light from the very beginning and the reason I fought so hard to become a different person. You will never understand how your existence changed my life. It has been an honor and a privilege to be chosen to be your mom.

Clark, without your faith in me, this book would not exist. You have been my driving force since day one. You believed in me and this book when I couldn't, and because of your faith, I kept going. You have encouraged me, supported me, and been so patient with me and this book for the past three years. When I look at you, I see so many attributes of Jesus, and I am so proud of the man you've become. It has been a blessing to be your wife.

Steude, you have helped me walk through this journey the past twenty years, and I am certain that without you, I could not have grown into who I am today. Thank you for being my friend, my counselor, my role model, and an earthly father figure. My life is much richer because you have been a part of it.

Amanda, you have been a godsend. Second to Clark, without you, this book would not be here today. I handed you the equivalent of a broken five-thousand-piece puzzle, and I asked you to fix it. You took my messy run-on sentences with bad grammar and no punctuation and turned it into a beautiful story. When I couldn't find the words to explain or express something, you always had the answer. You were so patient with me on rewrite after rewrite after rewrite. I don't know how you did it, but I will forever be grateful. You are truly amazing, and I thank God for you.

FOREWORD

After practicing psychiatry for more than forty-five years, it is a truth to me that we are all struggling to deal with a hole in our deepest being. It is lonely and empty. Healthy families help us cope with the pain. Less functional families teach us ways to pretend around it. Abusive families seem to add their anguish to ours, and they chip away at our souls, murdering parts of us.

As we struggle to deal with the emptiness, we search for answers. We try to fill the emptiness from without, trying to gain a sense of being lovable. We change ourselves based on what society and family show us, which is often lies. Even more destructive are the lies we tell ourselves in our search for truth. We get further from the person God created us to be.

This book tells of one person's struggle to find truth, *her* truth. Kristie has an active and beautiful mind, but it is sometimes her own worst enemy. She courageously lets us into her hopes, her fears, and her decades-long search for truth and even survival as a person. She shows how she would run in fear from the truth that her husband wasn't the answer—even as she tried to make him into her answer—and then she vows to never need him or anyone else. Being vulnerable is an anathema for her. She finally becomes guided spiritually and leaves the role of wife and mother, striking out on her own to find truth. She assumes her marriage is over, but in her search for truth, she becomes a person as God intended, and she finds some ultimate truths that pertain to us all.

Her answers may not be your answers, but her pathway should be helpful for all. I know Kristie. I wish you could know her too. Reading this book will be a delightful and occasionally uncomfortable journey into the person of Kristie. I have found her story meaningful and fascinating, and I trust you will enjoy sharing the experience.

—Phil Steude, MD
Board-certified in child, adolescent, and adult psychiatry

INTRODUCTION

I sat at home alone on thirteen acres with a very needy four-year-old when the world shut down. We had just moved to a new town two hours away from all our friends and family. Clark was considered an essential worker and could not stay home with me like every other husband I saw on social media. Oh, how I envied those wives! It had been a long time since I had been a stay-at-home mom, and with the world closed down, I thought I was about to lose my mind.

Clark barely made it through the door most days before I proclaimed, "It's your turn," and then I made my way out. I even met him on the porch some days and said, "She's had dinner but needs a bath." And then I would head out to my "she shed" to finish unpacking.

The problem started after I had everything unpacked. *What do I do now? How do I still leave the house when COVID has shut down the world?* Listen, don't judge. I needed quiet time. I needed time to think. I am an introvert on the verge of believing Clark and I had just made the biggest mistake of our life by basically selling everything we had, quitting my job of nineteen years, and moving to a farm. *I am a city girl! What in the world?* We told ourselves we were minimizing. I would be a stay-at-home mom who grows a garden, raises animals, and cares for a farm, even though that wasn't a life I ever aspired to have.

One night, while pretending to be busy in my she shed, I ran across a box I hadn't put away. I did not know what to do with this particular box because it had been untouched in my attic for the past seventeen years. Every season, I would see this box as I entered the attic to switch out clothes. I would stare at it quickly, almost as if it were forbidden, and look away. Season after season, year after year, I wondered if I should toss the box out or let it sit until the next. Surely it would make it to the trash someday, but not today, I always said.

Here it was, staring at me now. Feeling nostalgic and brave or extremely bored—I'm not sure which—I opened it. Every letter and card Clark and I had ever exchanged was in this box, along with some journals from an extremely hard time in our lives. That box contained a lot of dirty little secrets. That box held a lot of shame and embarrassment. That box held a lot of lies and guilt. No wonder I hadn't opened it in seventeen years.

But there I was, at two o'clock in the morning, sobbing on the floor of my she shed with all those notes. Each note had a memory that would take me back to that time and place; some made me giggle, and some made me shake my head, but those journals, girl, those journals tore me up. My insides shook just by rereading them.

Those journals took me back to those days, and it had been so long since I'd thought about them. Those were some of the darkest days of my life. The journey I had walked was the hardest I'd ever faced.

Even though I knew the ending, rereading those notes hurt so much. Remembering who we were really hurt, but we weren't those people anymore. Many nights, I sat out there on my knees and thanked God for delivering us. Clark and I walked through the fire, but we don't smell like smoke! Thank you, Jesus.

As I was reading one night, I giggled and thought, *This is what it would look like if a Hallmark movie collided with a Lifetime movie.* And then a wild thought ran through my head: *I should write a book about this.* And then I giggled some more—I would never write a book about my dirtiest little secrets.

That thought nagged at me for six months. It ate away at me and kept me awake at night. *We don't smell like smoke.* Most people don't know the fire Clark and I have been through because we don't smell like smoke. We don't smell like smoke because Jesus walked through the fire with us. Jesus also completely restored us, transformed our marriage, and reconciled us to him. How can I share this amazingness with the world if I'm too ashamed to talk about it because I'm afraid of what people might think? I can't.

God laid it on my heart that night that I can never be completely authentic with my testimony if I don't share this story because it is my biggest testimony. My story and Jesus are so deeply connected that if I don't tell one, I can't truly tell the other. God convicted me that night; that was exactly what was hindering me in my spiritual walk.

I took all those notes and journals, and I started writing. After a few months, I knew I needed to tell Clark I was writing this book about our marriage. I asked if there was anything he wanted me to leave out because I wanted to protect his privacy and be respectful of him.

He said, "And why must you write this book after seventeen years?"

"I feel like God is asking me to. In the past few months, he changed my heart about how I view that part of our life. For the longest time, I wouldn't allow myself to think about that season of our life, so I certainly wasn't going to talk about it. The feelings that accompanied those thoughts brought me so much shame and embarrassment. I thought the shame and embarrassment were rightfully due, but as I reread those notes and journals, instead of feeling shameful, all I could do was thank God for walking with us and delivering us. He made me realize I'm no longer in bondage to the enemy; my debt has been paid. It was paid a long time ago. I realized the shame and guilt I've been carrying is from the enemy, and I need to let it go."

"But, still, why write a book and expose our past?"

"I've had so many opportunities to share my story, our story, with other women in the same situation—women who are broken and hurting—but I didn't because of that fear and shame. My insecurities normally shut me down, but the few times I have shared this story, I saw barriers break and vulnerability fall. Those few times were some of the rawest, most real, most authentic conversations I've ever had. I didn't feel shamed or judged by them; I felt like I had offered them hope.

"Clark, God has convicted me not to let the enemy continue to hold power over me in this area, and I owe it to him to finally tell of the goodness that he has done in our lives and publicly give him the glory for it. If I can help one person, offer them some hope, and point them to the one true healer, then I've got to do it. People need to be reminded that God is the same today as he is in the Bible. He still performs miracles and continues using us, imperfect people, to tell of his goodness. If he can do this for our marriage, then he can do it for others too. They need to know that, and they need to see changed lives and a transformed marriage."

Clark looked at me so seriously at first, as if I had lost my mind, and then he smiled and said, "Tell them everything. I don't care. I'm not ashamed. Those choices led me here; glory is to God."

That's how the creation of this book came about, but it was not without many trials and struggles. This book has caused me so much heartache that I quit writing it four times—and there are about five different versions of it!

When I first started writing it, I got furious at my parents for the life they lived and how they raised their children. Seventeen years ago, when I processed my childhood with my therapist, all of us kids were a lot younger, and I didn't see the devastating, destructive life choices of my brothers as a result of that yet, but as I started writing, I saw it—and it made me mad. I was writing the story in a very aggressive tone, which I didn't like, and I quit writing.

A few months after that, my brother overdosed and died. Going back to my mom's house after many, many years for the funeral was so hard because of the many conflicting emotions, and I almost didn't go. I went, but I went like a bullet, ready to explode. I already had my mind set on that mentality. Maybe it was my protective, survival mode, I don't know, but the funny thing is my word for the year that year was love. I had been praying for God to teach me how to love like him, and this bullet mentality looked nothing like my prayer.

As I got there and started spending time with my mom and my family, I saw through adult lenses, mixed with some Jesus filters, that my mom was just as much a victim of her childhood as I had been. It had been fifteen years since I had spent any time with her, and fifteen years ago, I was not who I am today. I could not see anything other than myself: poor, pitiful me.

I had never thought about her or what her life had been like. With a different lens and perspective, I could filter things differently through my head and heart and offer her some grace. It was a real step toward forgiveness, which I'd never thought I'd have toward my mom, but God can do anything.

On my way home from the funeral, I knew I was ready to start this book again. However, once I got through the childhood part and started writing about Clark and me, I started having terrible anxiety. I would sit on my bed and cry. I would try to push through it, and I did most of the time, but it left me exhausted. For months, I would fall asleep by eight o'clock, feeling like I had run a marathon. Clark and I thought I was sick.

However, as soon as I got through the yucky parts of our life and started on the Jesus parts, everything returned to normal. The anxiety was gone, I had energy, and I felt lighter.

I went through another period where I quit writing altogether. Suddenly, the peace I felt about this book was gone. I kept hearing voices telling me, "No one will want to read this book; who cares about your story?" I started doubting that I had heard God correctly about writing this book. I began behaving like Gideon: *God, if you want me to write this book, show me a sign.* Nothing happened. I prayed and prayed. *God, if you want me to write this book, then give me peace. This book is for you, and you will do with it what you see fit—just give me the peace to finish it.*

A week later, a friend asked how the book was going. I shared my struggle with her. She confirmed what I already knew: the enemy was trying to throw me off course. He doesn't want us to do or say anything that will honor and glorify God, and he tries to attack us and make us second-guess ourselves. He's been doing it since the beginning of time, and he's not going to stop. We can't stop either. Spiritual warfare is real, and we can only fight it with spiritual weapons. I continued in prayer, asking God to guide my every word. He did, but he also allowed hiccups along the path. Those hiccups made me so angry, but now I know they were strengthening me and preparing me for what lies ahead.

I had one very loose rough draft done and felt so proud of myself, but when I started rereading it, I completely lost it. It was terrible! I cried to Clark that night, telling him I had wasted a year of my life, and there was no way I could tell the world this. I said, "I am not a writer! Why did you let me think I could do this?"

He looked at me and said, "I have faith in you. If you feel like God told you to do this, then don't you dare quit. Find a writing coach, find an editor, and find whoever you need to help you get this done—but just don't quit!"

"But, Clark, I am not a writer—and I'm not an author. You don't understand how bad this is."

"Kristie, you weren't a runner before you started running. You weren't a gardener before you started gardening. You weren't a mom until you had kids. Just do it. There is nothing you can't figure out when you want to. The question is, how bad do you want to?"

Clark's encouragement and faith in me pushed me to keep going. I found myself an editor, and months later, with the finish line in sight, I received a call that I had wondered about my entire life. "Kristie, your mom has died."

Her death hit me harder than I ever imagined, and I was stuck in bed, grieving for weeks. The book suddenly felt wrong, as if I were dishonoring her. So, once again, the book was put on hold.

One day, Clark came home from work to find me in bed again. He looked at me sincerely and said, "It's time to get up, Kristie. You need to write so you can process those feelings and begin healing."

He was right; it was time. As I started writing, a memory surfaced from my brother's funeral. My mom had told me, "I wish I had the courage to be as strong as you." That statement pierced my soul because I had never thought of myself as courageous. Most of my life had been merely putting one foot in front of the other, but that day, as I watched my mom unable to walk to my brother's casket, I understood that courage was putting one foot in front of the other.

And that was exactly what I needed to do during that season. As I wrote, I heard a little voice telling me my mom would be proud of me for having the courage to tell my story, even if it told parts of hers. A sense of peace returned to me to proceed with the book.

As I continued writing, I prayed for God's words to be louder than mine. I prayed that the story he wanted told would be told and not just the parts I wanted the world to know. I prayed that this book would be what he imagined it to be, no more, no less, with all the glory given to him.

Since this book is written from notes, letters, and journals from the past, some parts might not sound like me now, but they aren't supposed to. They are supposed to represent me during that time. I was lost, lonely, immature, and broken.

I took the letters, my best memories, and the memories of Clark to tell this story. I also returned to a therapist and asked for their opinion and memory to help me tell this as accurately, as honestly, and as raw as possible.

This book is a true story, and it tells parts of my childhood that land on other people's stories that aren't mine to tell. I tried to exclude those parts, but it just wasn't possible. So, to the best of my ability, I tried to dissect my part out of their stories where they intersected and overlapped. I tried to be extremely cautious and gentle with the stories I did tell out of respect for them.

You'll read in these pages an account of the lies I internalized from my childhood, how they affected my marriage for years, and the truths that God brought to me to set me free and redeem my marriage. You'll read about heartbreak, confusion, loss, hope, and healing. It's chronological, except where it isn't! Most of all, it's honest, as accurate as a flawed memory can recall, and—spoiler alert!—has such an ongoing happy ending because of the goodness and love of God.

I hope God speaks to you during this book and that you feel his mighty presence. He loves you so much. He thinks you are absolutely the greatest masterpiece he created you to be, and I do too. You are so much more than you might believe, and I pray that he reveals that to you through this book.

*   *   *

One generation commends your works to another; they tell of your
mighty acts. They speak of the glorious splendor of your majesty—
and I will meditate on your wonderful works. They tell of the power
of your awesome works—and I will proclaim your great deeds.
—Psalm 145:4–6

PART

I

THE COLOR OF CHILDHOOD

CHAPTER 1

THE FORMATION OF
FAULTY BELIEFS

Now I lay me down to sleep, I pray the Lord my soul to keep.
If I die before I wake, I pray the Lord my soul to take.

I stumbled onto my mamaw's porch as she was wrapping baby kittens in a plastic bag.

"What are you doing, Mamaw?"

"Throwing these kittens in the river."

"Why?"

"Because they're sick. I'm helping them die."

I was about six years old. I looked to my older cousin, hoping she had a solution. Instead, she just shrugged her shoulders. Without thinking, I grabbed that bag of kittens and took off running into the woods. I knew I would be in big trouble, but I didn't care; someone had to save them.

When I got back, my dad grabbed me by the shoulders and shook me so violently that I thought my head would snap. Back and forth, back and forth, he shook, all the while screaming, "Why do you do things like this? Why do you have to be so much trouble? This is exactly why no one likes you or wants to keep you!"

I just closed my eyes and prayed, pretending nothing was happening. "Now I lay me down to sleep, I pray the Lord my soul to keep. If I die before I wake, I pray the Lord my soul to take." That's all I knew to do, and that's the only prayer I knew.

I don't know where or from whom I learned that prayer, but I've prayed it every night as far back as I can remember. I didn't just pray it at night in bed; I prayed it during situations like that. Sometimes, I would pray in the car as my dad was driving us home drunk. I especially prayed during heated altercations between my parents or when I was the target of my dad's rage.

I wasn't concerned about the dying part. I just wanted to be sure that if I died, I would see that man Jesus I had heard so much about.

Now, listen. I didn't hear about Jesus in Sunday school or church, even though his name was used early Sunday mornings. Instead, I heard of him through violent threats and physical altercations, which were sometimes accompanied by the smell of alcohol, but not always.

God's name used in vain was a regular occurrence in our house.

Quite often, I would hear, "Oh, God!" followed by, "God can't help you now." That always left me wondering why God wouldn't help them. He helped me; he always calmed my heart when I prayed. *Maybe I should tell them about my prayer,* I thought.

I didn't dare, though, for fear he would be taken away just like everything else in my life. Instead, I began to pray my little prayer for others when bad things happened.

As a child, I always felt God's presence with me even though I knew nothing about him. I had both a fear and a love for him at an extremely early age. He was the safest part of me, always tucked away in my heart. At times, I felt like he was my imaginary friend, but he wasn't imaginary. He was real. I could feel him.

I had big feelings as a kid and was born into a family that didn't know how to handle their own, much less mine. I felt my feelings deep inside my bones, and I felt others' feelings too. This was a huge problem for the adults around me, and truth be told, it was a huge problem for me as well. Feeling the pain of those around me, plus my own, was a lot to handle. No adult understood my emotions, and they didn't know how to deal with me. Hence, someone was always saying, "Kristie is just too much for me to handle."

Like my Jesus, I learned my feelings had to be tucked away because they were perceived as bad, noncompliant, and disrespectful, and no adult in my family would be treated as such. I couldn't always keep them tucked away and hidden, and when they leaked out, was there a price to pay—just like with the kittens.

My childhood was colorful and eventful, but mainly in all the wrong ways. It's important for me to tell you about it though. Not because I need sympathy but because I want to show how the lies I received in my childhood affected the first decade of my marriage. God would heal and redeem, but I want you to see the challenge.

I grew up with my dad and stepmom in the coalfields of West Virginia until the age of twelve, when we moved to South Carolina. My favorite memories were the times I spent with my cousins. We were all oblivious to the destructive, dysfunctional behaviors of our families. We didn't know growing pot, making moonshine, and fighting chickens were not activities every family did. To us, it was like "take your kid to work day."

*   *   *

My mom's biological mother died a few days after giving birth to her, and she was passed around several times during childhood until her dad remarried. A few years after getting a new stepmom, her dad suddenly died. At fifteen, she left home, and she had already been married and divorced when she met and married my dad at sixteen. She soon became pregnant with me.

My dad had a pretty rough childhood also. His mom had him at fourteen and had four husbands before he was twelve. Mamaw was headstrong and not very nurturing. My dad never met his biological father, even though he raised another family in the area. I know this hurt my dad deeply, and he never figured out how to deal with the pain. So anger, rage, alcohol, and drugs became a part of him.

My parents divorced when I was two, and the only reason I've ever been given is that my grandmother cut down one of my dad's pot plants, and my mom didn't stop her.

I don't know how much time my parents spent with me during those first two years, but it definitely wasn't enough to bond with me. My parents were huge party people with alcohol and drug addictions, and neither was willing to give that up to take care of me. They would leave me with anyone willing to watch me. Mamaw eventually took me full-time.

Mamaw told me she had to beg my parents to come get me and buy me diapers and formula. She said she would have me for weeks before my parents called or came to see me.

I have very few scattered memories of life before age five, but I can remember when my parents remarried. I remember my mom showing up at my mamaw's house and asking if she could talk to my dad outside. I was so confused about why my mom was there that I darted outside as soon as my mamaw left the living room. I heard my mom say she was getting married; she asked if I could come. My dad got furious when he saw me and started hollering and cussing. I'm unsure if he was mad at my mom or me, but he grabbed my arm, dragged me inside, and slammed the door.

A few days later, I got up the nerve to ask if I could go to my mom's wedding, and my dad informed me that I couldn't because he was getting married, and it happened to be on the same day. My dad says he planned the date first, and my mom says he did it to spite her.

I vividly remember that after my dad remarried, Mamaw said, "Pack your clothes; you're going to live with your dad and Patty."

"Why can't I live here anymore?"

"Kristie, I got too many kids of my own to raise. It's time for someone else to raise you."

I started to cry. I didn't want to leave the only home I'd ever known.

Mamaw said, "Think of it this way: you are my wedding gift to them, and everyone loves a gift."

Life as I knew it changed that day. I felt like I was handed off to a new family. Without much warning, I went to live with a woman I didn't know, a dad I barely knew, and a new brother.

I don't think Patty and my daddy liked their gift because I heard them arguing that night about me living with them full-time. I suspected it was just as much of a surprise to them as it was to me. I didn't want to be there either, but hearing they didn't want me there hurt worse. It made me wonder why they didn't want me. What had I done to them? Why didn't my mom want me? And why didn't Mamaw want me anymore? Why didn't anyone want me, for that matter?

As I heard them arguing, I suddenly felt broken, like something was wrong with me. I felt so sad and lonely, a feeling I didn't remember having until that night.

That night became the introduction to the awareness of a wound deep inside me, an ache, a void, a missing piece. That night, I felt broken, and the pain hurt so badly. I would feel that same brokenness for the next twenty years. I would grow up feeling unwanted, unworthy, and unloved by the three main people in my life.

*   *   *

I loved to climb trees and wear boys' socks. I would go to my mom's house, and the first thing I would do is change clothes, put on my brother's long socks (the ones I could pull up to my knees), run outside with the trailer park kids, and climb a tree or play baseball. That was so much fun. I felt free, like the real me. My mom was very loving and affectionate toward me, but I didn't see her often. Maybe once a month on good months, but really like once every other month.

At any rate, my mom had started a new family. I remember asking her why I couldn't live with her, and she said, "Your dad says no," and that was it. There was no explanation or sadness in her voice. She spoke matter-of-factly—like he was the law. For his part, my dad made sure to let me know that she had moved on and forgotten about me.

There was a lot of hatred between my mom and dad—and Patty seemed to have an intense hatred for my mom as well. My dad wouldn't let me see my mom because he said she was doing things she shouldn't be doing, that she wouldn't take care of me, and that he didn't trust her. It never made sense to me because I hardly ever saw my dad either: he worked twelve-hour days during the week and didn't come home on the weekends much. He still liked to party.

I'm not sure Patty wanted to start raising someone else's kid full-time, but she did.

I was a very detached and misunderstood child. I didn't have a bond with anyone—no safe person. I wanted friends and people to like me. I knew very early on that I was different. I felt different, lonely, sad, and very serious. I didn't know how to loosen up or be fun.

Things bothered me that didn't seem to bother other people. How could I have fun when so many bad things were always happening around me? (And I'm not just talking about hurting animals). I had difficulty looking away from things that seemed unfair or not right. I frequently heard, "Get over it," "Quit crying and toughen up," and "Quit worrying about other people." I never understood how to do any of those things, though.

Over and over, I heard, "Why can't you be like everyone else?" and "Why can't you just do what you're told?"

If I didn't feel different, I would have surely known it because everyone talked about it.

"Why does Kristie talk so much?"

"Why is Kristie so bossy?"

"Why doesn't Kristie listen?"

"Why is Kristie so bad?"

I always heard everyone talking about me, but never once did anyone ask me how I felt or what was going on inside my mind. Instead, as a kid, when I would hear this, I would get sad and try to figure out what I could do better to make them stop talking about me. I really had no idea why I talked so much except that I liked people.

I also never understood how or why everyone thought I was so bossy. I liked to help people, and I was fixated on doing the right things the right way. When someone wasn't doing what they were supposed to, I would tell them what they were doing wrong and how to fix it. If they listened, great. It made me feel good to know I had helped them. If they didn't listen, I told on them. In my head, I didn't want them to get in trouble. I tried to save them from trouble, but neither the kids, the adults, nor the teachers seemed to understand that.

Everyone kept telling me I didn't listen, but I listened. I did things I didn't want to do, I did things I believed were wrong or unfair, and I said things I didn't want to say, but I did them because I listened.

Sometimes, though, things meant so much to me that I couldn't listen, so I did what I thought was right, like with those kittens.

In my adolescent mind, I couldn't understand why everyone wasn't concerned about those kittens, a black eye, a busted head, or anything else that worried me greatly. I was concerned though, and they mattered. Hurt people and animals mattered enough to me that I would take the spanking if I thought it might help the situation.

As a result, in my family, I was deemed the bad kid. And at school, I was the kid who talked too much, didn't pay attention, and couldn't sit still. I tried to observe how the other kids acted and mimicked that. I grew up learning to watch and observe what worked for others and to do that, be that, and act like that. I never grew into myself because I spent my childhood trying to be like the other kids, just like they told me to.

*   *   *

When I was around eight, my mom went missing out of my life for a year, and then she suddenly resurfaced at my door. I was so excited to see her standing there, but my dad wouldn't let me talk to her. I ran to the window to look out. I heard her saying, "Darrell, please just let me see her for a few minutes." He refused and kept telling her to get off his property. "Five minutes, Darrell, just five minutes."

Quickly, I saw him pick her up, carry her back to her car, throw her in, turn around, and walk back inside.

I ran to the door and screamed, "I want to see my mom."

He said, "She didn't even ask to see you."

She called several times for the next few weeks until my dad finally let me talk to her. He agreed to let me see her the upcoming Saturday. I was ecstatic! I could not wait to see her.

On Saturday morning, I got up early, dressed, and waited for the clock to read 9:00. Finally, she should be here any minute. Nine, ten, and eleven rolled around, and no Mom.

My dad came out on the porch and said, "Come inside; she ain't coming."

I didn't believe him. "She's coming; she's just running late." *Something had to have happened because she wanted to see me.*

He shook his head and said, "She ain't coming, Kristie. She's got more important things to do."

I dialed her number at least a hundred times that day, and finally, around nine o'clock that night, she answered.

"Hello?"

"Mom! Where have you been? I've been waiting on you all day."

"Oh, sis, was that today? I totally forgot. Charles got paid for some work he did, and we went grocery shopping."

"I waited for you all day."

"I'm sorry, sis. Ask your dad if I can come next weekend."

As soon as I hung up the phone, my dad said, "I told you she had more important things to do."

My dad's words hurt more than what my mom had done. My dad was right; she did have more important things to do. I wasn't important. I lay in bed and wondered how she could have forgotten about me. How was I not more important than groceries? Couldn't she have gone grocery shopping another time? She never gets to see me, wasn't I more important than groceries? Clearly, I wasn't important at all.

Marriage would turn out to be no different. I never felt chosen. Clark married me because we had a baby, and his parents told him it was the right thing to do. At eighteen, neither of us knew of any other option. So I went into the marriage feeling sorry that Clark—just like everyone else—had gotten stuck with me.

This was the first lie wedged deep into my soul from childhood: I'm not wanted. I'm inconvenient. I'm not good enough. I'm not important enough.

*   *   *

As a kid, all I knew about love was it was a feeling that made you happy or sad. From what I had watched in my dad and stepmom's marriage, love was doing things right. Notice I didn't say, "Doing the right thing." I said, "Doing things right." Doing things right that were acceptable and pleasing made you lovable. My dad would be happy and nice if I did what he told me to do correctly. Happy and nice equated to love. The only problem was that we hardly ever did anything right the first time, so rarely was anyone happy or nice in my family.

I learned that my role in life was not to be heard or make any disruptions to anyone's life.

My dad was a functioning alcoholic. He worked in the coal mines, and when he wasn't working, he was drinking. Drinking would start Friday night and continue through Sunday night. My dad was a sloppy, mean, violent drunk. He would come home in the early morning hours and wake us up, dragging us out of bed just because he could, I guess. I really don't know why he did that.

He would come home hungry, and if he couldn't find anything to eat, he would throw everything out of the cabinets and fridge and demand Patty fix him something to eat. Depending on his mood, she would either do it right, and he would eat and go to bed, or she would do it wrong, and a physical altercation would occur.

Waking up and seeing our house trashed was normal: tables turned over or broken, the phone yanked off the wall and smashed, and dishes shattered on the floor. Whatever was within his sight would be trashed.

The next morning, one of three things always happened: Patty already had the place cleaned up, Patty was gone, or Patty was still in bed, most likely hurt from the physical altercation—so I cleaned up for her. I learned to clean up as quickly as possible; the longer my dad had to see the mess, the longer he stayed aggravated.

I started seeing a pattern with my dad: he only spoke kindly to me when I was cleaning up his messes. He would praise me for being such a good helper and tell me how everyone likes a good girl. He would point out how Patty wasn't being good and how she had made him do all of this.

I didn't like to see the fights or clean up the mess, but I did look forward to my dad's attention. I learned that attention was love—and love was earned by cleaning up other people's messes.

When my dad would do something wrong, it was always someone else's fault, whether they were involved or not. It was never his fault, and he never took responsibility for his actions. Instead, he had a way of manipulating you into believing it was your fault. Therefore, it was your responsibility to make things right, "earn back his love," or "earn back his trust" to make him feel better about his behavior.

One morning, he came home drunk and announced, "Don't bother looking for your cat. I threw it over the mountain."

I began crying.

He started hollering, "Don't be crying at me. Cry at your own self or that *blankety-blank* cat. I wouldn't have had to do it if it weren't at my feet."

I was sobbing uncontrollably.

"How do you think this makes me feel? You should be more concerned about me and how I feel than that cat."

Speechless and still crying.

"Look at me," he said as he pounded the table. "Do you think I wanted to do that?"

I didn't answer.

He pounded the table again and screamed, "Do you really think I wanted to do that?"

I shook my head no.

"Exactly! This is not my fault. It's your cat, so why are you acting this way? Don't you love me?"

I stood there without answering because I knew anything I said would be wrong.

"No, you don't love me. If you loved me, this wouldn't have happened. You're just like your mom, always causing me to do stuff and then crying to make it look like it's my fault."

I knew "just like your mom" meant I couldn't do anything right and wouldn't amount to anything. I'd heard that enough times to know.

"You sit here until you figure out how to show me you love me and appreciate what I do for you."

He walked toward me, getting so close I could smell his breath, and said, "I could have given you away just like your mom, and I probably should have."

And then he turned and walked out of the room as if he were the victim—and his words hadn't just crushed my soul.

*   *   *

The word *love* confused me because my mom was the only one who told me she loved me, yet she didn't really act like it. I don't think I grew up ever knowing what that word was supposed to mean. My dad never used the word *love* as a term of endearment; for him, it was a tool of manipulation.

"If you love me, you will do this."

"If you loved me, you wouldn't have done that."

"Your mom doesn't love you because she won't raise you."

"If you acted right, I might love you."

My dad used the word against me more than he used it for me. I began to feel as if it was a dirty four-letter word.

As a kid, I understood love was earned. You earn love from your behavior, actions, and words. The way you make other people feel makes you loved. If you make them feel good about themselves, you were good and loved. If you did or said something that made them feel bad, then you were bad and definitely not loved.

To be loved meant you had been good enough to earn it. Love was tangible, though. You had it until you messed up, and then it was taken back from you. And it was your job to earn it back. If you didn't earn it back, you weren't loved.

As I got older, I understood love to be something you do; it was production-based. It was still earned, but it had to be physically worked for.

My dad would say he loved me because he went to work for me. If he didn't love me, he would stay home like the other deadbeat dads who didn't love their kids. And since he "loved" me, it was my job to pay him back for his love. Paying him back and earning his love meant being productive. Being idle was unacceptable. If you weren't at school, you better be working at home to pay him back for the hours he worked for you. He had my mind so programmed out of fear that even if I had everything done, when I heard his truck pull into the driveway, I jumped up and pretended to be busy.

I viewed being loved and being happy as the same thing. If someone loved you, it was their job to make you happy. I had no idea you could be unhappy with someone but still love them because being loved and happy were such extreme emotions in my house. They went together and were conditional. Some days, I may be loved; others, I may not.

In essence, my job was to figure out how to be loved and do it correctly. In return, my happiness was a gift allotted back to me, determined by how well I did that job.

Basically, my happiness was based on whether I did my job well and whether those around me were happy. If they were pleased, then I had earned the right to be loved, and being loved meant I should be happy—because it was a gift. Being loved also brought you value.

Of course, earning the right to be loved could change from minute to minute. Therefore, I grew up believing love was transactional and must be earned. This belief reinforced that I was not loved for who I was but for what I did. Since I had a huge need to be loved, I always tried to perform and be good. This belief made me think that my works would be the deliverer of my love. And the better my works were, the more love I would receive. Did I carry this belief into my marriage? You bet I did! Was I aware of it? Absolutely not. Would it cause problems? One hundred percent.

This was the second great lie of my childhood: Love must be earned. I have to please everyone in order to be loved or cared for.

> *My job was to figure out how to be loved.*

* * *

My dad dictated my entire childhood. I didn't know how to make decisions because I was never really allowed to make them. As kids, we weren't allowed to pick out our clothes, book bag, or lunchbox. We were not involved in any decision-making process. We were just happy that we got new clothes or shoes or a book bag.

Even on the rare occasions when we were "allowed" to make a decision, it was a ruse: we had to "make" the decision the adult wanted.

In fourth grade, I was taken to the store and told I could pick any shoes I wanted. I picked out a pair of white high-top Reeboks with two Velcro straps at the top—the shoes everyone wore. I was so excited that I was getting those shoes. I got to try them on and everything—only to be told to take them off immediately because they were too expensive.

"Kristie, why can't you appreciate that you're getting new shoes and not pick out the most expensive ones?"

I started to cry. I hadn't meant to be unappreciative. I didn't even know the price of the shoes. After causing a scene in the store, I was told we could get them—but don't dare think of asking for another thing, ever! I got those shoes, and for the entire year I wore them, I remembered how selfish I was for picking out such expensive shoes. I wondered every day if I had taken money away from our bills. Every single time I put on those shoes, I felt guilty.

I quickly understood the difference between a decision and an expectation; a decision is a choice, and an expectation is expected. Decisions might have been presented, but the correct answer was expected; otherwise, there would be consequences.

When presented with a decision, I learned how to ask questions to determine what choice I thought was expected.

Most of the time, though, I was told what to do before I even had the chance to ask, which I liked. If I knew what was expected, I could do it without messing up.

Making a decision alone, though, scared me. In fifth grade, I wrote a paper in English about my mom having my twin brothers. My teacher bragged about how well the paper was written and asked me to read it aloud to the class. I was so excited about this that I told Patty. She was furious and told my dad. They said I wasn't allowed to write about my mom and brothers because they didn't live in our house and were not my family. I was told under no circumstance was I allowed to read that paper to the class, and to ensure I didn't, Patty came to my school the next day and demanded my English teacher give the paper to her.

My dad asked, "How pathetic are you to write about brothers you don't even have?"

I knew that really wasn't a question, so I didn't reply. I just hung my head low and tried to hold back the tears.

Constantly feeling inadequate about making good decisions and fearful of the outcome developed fear in me that caused so much anxiety in my adolescent heart.

This fear plunged me into becoming a people pleaser with no self-agency. Self-agency is the ability to self-advocate and make wise decisions that are consistent with the life you want. It's a sense of self-efficacy.

My therapist later told me that self-agency develops in childhood, and parents play a crucial role in helping children build this critical quality. If they are never allowed to practice decision-making, children are more likely to become people pleasers.

Did this affect my marriage with Clark? You bet it did.

This was the lie: I am incapable of making my own decisions. I have no self-agency.

*   *   *

If any of you lacks wisdom, you should ask God, who gives generously
to all without finding fault, and it will be given to you.
—James 1:5

*   *   *

Once, on the ride home from my mom's house, I begged her to ask my dad if I could live with her. She told me I would need to be the one who asked him.

I started crying because I knew how my dad reacted whenever I brought up my mom's name, and if he knew I wanted to live with her, he would explode on me.

"Mom, please ask him, please! I'm begging you. They all hate me and are mean to me."

I was a kid, and she was my mom. I didn't understand why she wouldn't do this for me. I begged and begged the whole ride home. She finally said pretty sternly, "You need to be the one to ask him."

When we got to my dad's house, the first thing my dad said was, "What did your mom do to make you cry?"

"Nothing."

"Why are you crying?"

I looked toward my mom.

My dad yelled, "What did you do to make her cry?"

My mom looked up from the ground and shyly said, "Darrell, she wants to live with me."

I could see the look change on my dad's face and knew this wouldn't go well.

He said, "Get out of my house—and never come back. Don't you ever call her again. I told you that you could see her, but if you started filling her head with promises you can't keep, you can't see her."

My mom got in her car without even a goodbye to me.

Later that week, my dad woke me up and said, "Put on a dress; we've got somewhere to go."

While driving, he told me we would see a judge to ensure my mom never tried to take me away from him again. I didn't understand because my mom wasn't trying to take me away. I *wanted* to live with her, but I didn't dare say that. I was too scared.

We got to court, and my mom was there. I was so excited to see her. I ran over to her, and as she leaned down to hug me, she whispered in my ear, "If you want to live with me, you have to tell the judge."

We sat there forever. I was working up the courage so that when I heard our name called, I would be brave enough to tell the judge what I wanted. But when they called our name, they said, "Mrs. Dawson, Do you have an attorney present?"

"No."

"The court will give you six weeks to find one and reschedule this hearing." And we left.

We returned to court six weeks later, but my mom didn't show up. I didn't hear from her for months after that. When I finally saw her, she told me she didn't have the money for an attorney.

"Does that mean I have to live with my dad?"

She nodded and said, "When you turn twelve, you will be old enough to tell a judge who you want to live with."

She told me she loved me and would see me every weekend and said things would be okay.

I told her things were not okay.

She hushed me and said, "You will be fine."

"But can you borrow the money?"

"No."

"But, Mom ..."

"Kristie, I can't. This is just how it is. There is no reason for us to talk about it anymore."

My heart was broken, and I was so confused. Why was my dad fighting for me if he didn't want me? And if my mom wanted me, why wasn't she?

As a child, there was always this hole in my heart, this void in my life. I always felt sad. For the longest time, I felt it to be for my mom. I longed for her to want me, to choose me, to love me. But that was never going to happen.

* * *

The day I turned twelve, I called my mom. "Mom, I am twelve today; I can live with you as you said."

"Sis, what are you talking about?"

"Mom, you told me I could come live with you when I turned twelve."

"Live with me, well … um … I mean, you've lived with your dad for so long now."

"I know, but I'm twelve now and want to live with you."

"Kristie, I don't know if your dad will like that."

"Mom, don't you want me?"

"Kristie, I want you, but you are twelve now; you will be on your own soon, and besides, I have three kids now and no room for you in my house."

"You don't want me." *My dad was right all along; she had never wanted me.*

"Kristie, I want you. I love you."

"You may love me, but you have never wanted me." *I doubt she even loves me.* I hung up.

And if all that wasn't proof enough for my aching heart, there was the incident when I was fourteen and missed the school bus one afternoon.

I tried calling home, but there was no answer. I saw a guy who lived in the neighborhood and asked if he could give me a ride. When we turned onto my street, and I saw my dad's blue truck waiting at the bus stop, I knew something bad was about to happen.

As I got in his truck, I tried to explain what had happened, but he wouldn't let me finish. He started hollering and cussing at me, telling me I knew I wasn't allowed in any boy's car. He was accusing me of doing all kinds of things, and as I was trying to tell him nothing like that had happened and that I had tried to call several times from school, which he could see from caller ID, he became furious and started beating me.

I made it inside the house and collapsed onto the floor. I remained there until nighttime. The following morning, pain shot through my body as I walked into the bathroom. I almost fainted when I saw my face in the mirror. No wonder I felt so much pain.

I stood in the shower and cried because of the physical pain, and because I didn't know what to do. There was no way I could go to school looking like this, plus I could barely move. I definitely couldn't maneuver my body into a school desk.

When I heard my dad's truck leave, I called my mom, the only person I thought would know what to do. "Mom, I need your help. My dad beat me last night, and I can barely walk."

"Aw, sis, is it that bad?"

Shocked by the question, I replied, "Yes, Mom, it is that bad. You know what he is capable of."

Her voice lowered, and she said, "Yeah, I know what he's capable of."

"Mom, will you come get me?"

"Oh, sis, give him a day or two. He will cool off, and everything will be fine."

"Mom, I can't walk. I can't even stand up straight. My ribs hurt. My entire body hurts."

She said, "I know how that feels."

Silence. I was holding back tears. *I can't believe she isn't rushing to get me.* "Mom, I probably need to go to the doctor."

"You can't go to the doctor. He will get in trouble."

"He needs to get in trouble for what he did. Besides, why do you care? He hates you."

The line went utterly silent. *What is going on here? Doesn't she care even a little?*

She interrupted the silence. "Do you have any Tylenol?"

I felt anger rising inside of me. "Are you kidding me, Mom? Tylenol?"

"Kristie, what do you want me to do?"

"I want you to come get me."

"Oh, I can't do that."

My heart dropped. "Why not?"

"Sis, I'll get in trouble for kidnapping."

"Mom, if anyone sees me, they will clearly understand why you took me, and if anyone sees me, he will go to jail, so I don't think you have to worry about kidnapping."

"Oh, sis, is it that serious?"

"Mom, I am black and blue. I can't go to school. I can't even sit up straight, and I can barely walk. What do you not understand about what I'm saying? I need you. I don't know what else to do."

She sat there for a minute and said, "Kristie, I am sorry, but I can't get involved; he will hurt me too."

In desperation, I screamed, "Mom, what am I supposed to do?"

"I don't know, sis. I don't know."

My head was spinning. I couldn't even think of how to respond. What I understood was she wasn't coming to help me—never have and never will. Despite her track record, this shocked me.

I hung up on her. She wasn't going to sacrifice her peace, her life, or her comfort for me. *She isn't scared of him; she just doesn't want to be bothered. She hasn't ever helped me or come to my rescue. She hasn't ever fought for me. Why would I expect her to now?*

Because I'm sitting here half-dead?

Well, clearly, that doesn't matter either.

My dad might have hurt my body, but my mom destroyed my spirit and broke my heart. The reality that no one would ever show up for me, love me, choose me, or help me became so apparent in the pit of my soul that it hurt just to breathe. The mental and physical pain hurt so bad that I couldn't imagine either ever healing.

The lie: I was not worthy of sacrifice.

*   *   *

Though my father and mother forsake me, the Lord will receive me.
—Psalm 27:10

*   *   *

After my dad beat me, I sat in bed for three days, unable to move physically. At first, I just lay there feeling sorry for myself. *No one loves me. No one cares about me. No one is ever here for me. I can't depend on anyone. No one is reliable. I am the only person who will ever take care of me.*

As I sat there contemplating life, childhood scenes replayed through my mind. I knew what was expected of me. Take care of myself ... but don't get into trouble. Clean up after the adults ... but don't make a mess. Figure out and take care of what I need ... but don't ask for help.

It was evident that I couldn't rely on anyone. I had yet to be helped; why would that change now? If I wanted help, I would have to help myself.

That day I made a list of rules for myself in my diary:

- I will not be stuck in a marriage.
- No man will ever hit me again.
- I will not become dependent on anyone in life. I will take care of myself. I don't need anyone.
- No one will control me or tell me what to do.
- I won't be the type of mother my mom is.
- I will not drink or do drugs like my parents.
- I will not ask for help because that makes you weak, and weak people lose.
- I will not be anything like my dad, my mom, or Patty.
- I will do everything opposite of my dad, Patty, and my mom.

And that's just what I did. A part of my heart hardened during that time, but I knew I had to stuff my feelings and expectations of others down deep or continue to feel the pain. The pain made you weak and kept you vulnerable, and I would become neither of those. If I was in control of my feelings, no one could hurt me.

It's no wonder the first decade of my marriage was such a difficult season. And it's no wonder the journey of healing and redemption would take a long time.

The big lie from my childhood? Self-reliance. I must care for myself without depending on anyone else.

*   *   *

What was the accumulated result of these beliefs? Emptiness. I did not grow up feeling loved or knowing God, but I certainly felt the emptiness. The void was there, and the longing for something more was always present. For me, the emptiness manifested through a longing to be loved. I thought if I were ever loved properly, all would finally be good in my life. I would never feel the emptiness again; it would all go away.

I couldn't have been more wrong. Those beliefs hardened my heart and wounded me way more than they protected me. I entered marriage, and parenting, hobbled with some serious lies that would continue to severely damage pretty much every relationship in my life. I wanted to be loved, seen, accepted, cherished, and respected—and I had no clue how those things would happen.

CHAPTER 2

THE RIGHT THING TO DO

Clark was my high school sweetheart and the love of my life. Even though we started dating at the tender age of fourteen, he loved me in a way I had never been loved before. He accepted me without conditions. The things I said were important. The things I wanted, he got. He made me feel special. I felt seen, valued, and heard. I didn't know this was an option in a relationship because I had spent my childhood and adolescent days trying to be seen but not heard. With Clark, I had a voice—and it mattered.

When we first started dating, I was a huge people pleaser, but I didn't know how to be any other way. Honestly, I didn't even realize that about myself until Clark picked up on it.

Clark saw that I wasn't used to making my own decisions and tried to encourage me to make them, but he could tell how difficult that was for me. He started giving me the assignment of deciding where I wanted to go or what I wanted to eat every other time the decision needed to be made.

At first, it was so daunting. I was afraid he would get upset and love me less if I gave an answer he didn't like or want, but that never happened. He always acted as if I made the best choice possible and was very happy to oblige.

Clark was the first person who ever spent time with me, got to know me, and encouraged me to be me. I felt worthy just because he loved me.

As the years passed, Clark and I behaved like we were the only two people on the planet. He would pick me up for school in the mornings and bring me home. We met between classes, and he would walk me to the next one. We ate lunch together and shared a locker because two would take too much time. We hung out exclusively on the weekends and didn't participate in school activities or events.

It was Kristie and Clark, from morning to dark, for three years. Looking back now, I can see how this stunted a huge growth in my adolescent development.

*　*　*

Clark's life was so different than mine. He grew up in South Carolina in a Christian home with both of his parents. He had a traditional southern upbringing, where all the aunts, uncles, and cousins met at the grandparents' house, and everyone got along ever so beautifully.

It blew my mind the first time I went to a holiday dinner at Nanny's house with Clark. I first noticed that everyone was so kind, inviting, and accepting.

Next, I realized that everyone stayed sober and calm the entire time. That seemed strange to me. At the dinner table, everyone was sincerely engaged in how the others were doing. As they talked and laughed and carried on, it amazed me. There was no gossip or judgment, no cussing or alcohol. It reminded me of a scene out of a Hallmark movie.

The conversations that took place included me, which shocked me. I had never been invited into an adult conversation. I liked it, but it made me realize I didn't know how to have an intelligent conversation with an adult. Most of my answers were, "I don't know." I could feel my face turning bright red and burning from the attention. I felt so out of place, but I longed to belong.

On the drive home that night, I asked Clark if every dinner or gathering was like that.

He said, "Normally."

I immediately knew two things: I wanted to become a part of this family, and I wanted a family of my own just like this one day.

*　*　*

On my sixteenth birthday, Clark took me to the mall and told me to pick out any dress and shoes I wanted. He said, "We have dinner plans tonight at the Melting Pot, and I thought it would be fun if we dressed up."

No one had ever taken me to the mall and told me I could pick out anything I wanted. I felt like Cinderella with her fairy godmother. I was overwhelmed but excited. I went to the women's dresses instead of the juniors' section. I wanted to look sophisticated and classy, and I wanted something that Clark would like.

I had never been to a fancy restaurant. I was very intimidated and afraid I would mess up. Clark pulled my chair out for me, and we used those cloth napkins. *Fancy*, I thought.

We talked for hours, so immersed in our own little world that we didn't realize the restaurant was closing.

Clark was so effortless to talk to, and I loved him. That night, I knew I wanted to spend the rest of my life with him.

Right before we left the restaurant, he told me he was going to Nashville Auto Diesel College in the summer.

I felt my stomach turn; the thought of him leaving for college had never crossed my mind. It had been such a magical night, and I felt a tear run down my face. "Let's talk about this later. Tonight is a happy night. Please don't ruin it."

He smiled and nodded as if he understood.

We had been together for two years, and I knew he loved me; his behavior reflected it. I felt safe with him; he was the first person I had ever trusted. He was so kind and patient with me. He laughed at the silly things I did and said, and he looked over my flaws and deficits, just like that night when he told me to close my mouth while chewing.

He took me home, and as we said goodbye, I said, "This was the very best birthday I've ever had with my very best friend."

He smiled and said, "You deserve to have many more very best birthdays."

"And I hope you're around for every single one."

He laughed, but he didn't reply.

Does he want to be around for all of them? Maybe he doesn't. That might be what the college conversation is about. Maybe he thinks we should end things now since he's leaving for college in a few months. My insides were starting to panic.

Clark interrupted my thoughts by saying, "That dress looked good on you tonight."

I giggled nervously. Since I didn't know how to respond appropriately to a compliment, I said, "Even while chewing with my mouth open?"

"*Especially* while chewing with your mouth open."

We giggled again. The comment made my heart smile. *He loves me. We're good. There's no need to worry.*

*　*　*

As Christmas was approaching, Clark asked me what I wanted.

"I don't want anything; you buy me so much already."

"What is something you would like?"

I thought for a moment and blurted out, "A kitten."

Clark giggled at my request and said, "A kitten, of course."

Christmas Eve rolled around, and we exchanged gifts. We had both gotten each other a silk shirt. Don't laugh! This was 1993, and silk shirts were *the* thing!

His was blue, and mine was purple. We laughed about buying each other the same gift, but we always did stuff like that. He would finish my sentences, or I would say, "I was just thinking the same thing." We were so in sync that I couldn't imagine my life without him. I truly felt like he completed me; he certainly filled the emptiness I had lived with for so long.

When I walked him to his truck that night, he handed me his gift and told me to put it on the passenger side. I opened the door, and a little white and black kitten was in a box. He looked at me and said, "Merry Christmas."

Tears came to my eyes. He heard me, and it mattered. *This is the nicest thing anyone has ever done for me.*

It seemed like when I was happy, that made Clark happy. I was dumbstruck by how much he cared about me. He was the only good thing in my life.

* * *

However, in the blink of an eye, it all ended. Clark went to college the summer before my senior year. I dreaded every minute as it got closer to move-in day. I started picking fights with him, hoping he would break up with me so it wouldn't hurt as bad when he left. He saw right through it and was just as patient and understanding as he had always been.

I was not ready for this goodbye thing. We never got around to having that college conversation. I couldn't. Clark tried, but I would change the subject whenever he brought it up. I was just fine ignoring the fact that the day would eventually arrive. I was hopeful that it might not come true if I pretended long enough.

I rode to Nashville with him and his parents. I wanted every last minute I could have with him. I felt paralyzed the entire drive there—my body heavy, my mind foggy. It felt like I was going to a funeral. I couldn't comprehend leaving him there and coming home alone. I wasn't interested in starting a life without him and did not know how to. We were so enmeshed that I didn't know where he ended, and I began.

The weekend went by so fast; ready or not, it was goodbye time. Standing there and saying goodbye was tougher than I imagined; I just froze. All eyes were on me, and I couldn't move or speak. I felt my insides getting tingly and knotting up. My face was starting to get hot and flush. *Don't cry. Be strong. Please, Kristie, don't cry.*

Clark stepped toward me and grabbed my arm. "Come here, silly." He wrapped me in his arms and said, "It's okay. I'll see you soon. It will be fine, we will get through this."

I swear, he always had a way of knowing exactly what I was feeling and what I needed to hear.

* * *

When I returned home, I became depressed. I felt like a part of me was missing. I would stay in bed for hours and cry. My heart physically hurt; I had no idea love could hurt so bad. I was shocked by this feeling. I knew I would miss him, but I did not anticipate feeling like my heart had been ripped from my chest.

Some days, I felt like I could barely breathe. The feelings hurt so bad and would come out of nowhere. No matter how hard I tried, I couldn't control them, much less make them stop.

I walked through the days on autopilot, doing only what I knew out of habit: get up, go to work, come home, and go straight to bed. That's all I did because I couldn't figure out what else I was supposed to do with me or my time. Clark was what made me. I had no sense of who I was apart from him.

Staying connected to Clark—or trying to—was the only thing that made me feel normal. I craved him; he was like a drug running through my blood. I couldn't eat or sleep, and I lost twenty pounds.

I was constantly writing and calling him. (Back in 1994, we still wrote notes and mailed them!) I felt like I was constantly bleeding, and Clark was the only Band-Aid. I became obsessed with where he was and what he was doing whenever he didn't answer the phone. I was becoming obsessed with him and didn't even realize what was happening.

* * *

The idols of the nations are silver and gold, made by human hands.
They have mouths, but cannot speak, eyes, but cannot see. They have
ears, but cannot hear, nor is there breath in their mouths. Those who
make them will be like them, and so will all who trust in them.
—Psalm 135:15–18

* * *

If three months without Clark seemed excruciating, returning to school was much worse. School reminded me that Clark chose to leave me, which stung differently. Walking through the halls alone with no friends and no one to eat lunch with made me feel pathetic, and I became angry that I had let myself become so isolated and dependent on someone.

I didn't like that feeling, and I despised the fact that Clark was having the time of his life despite me sitting at home by the phone, waiting for him to call.

Initially, we talked every afternoon at four o'clock, but as the months went by, that time got later and later. I lived for our calls, but he didn't. *Why?* That hurt my heart, which made me angrier.

One day, after talking for only fifteen minutes, he said he needed to go because he was tired. I had waited to speak with him all day, and he hardly seemed to care. I lost my temper, accusing him of not caring about me, and we hung up angry. An hour later, after I calmed down and felt terrible about my behavior, I called to apologize—only to learn he'd gone out for the night. *Wait, what? He isn't tired at all, and he's not in bed.* Oh, man, I was so furious. The next day, I broke up with him via voicemail.

You better believe he called back then, but I avoided his calls for two weeks. Of course, that only made things worse. Eventually, by the time we finally talked, we were both so upset at the other's behavior that we agreed that breaking up was for the best. It seemed like a mutual breakup, but I was devastated. I had hoped that Clark would have put up a fight not to end our three-year relationship, but he didn't.

As the weeks rolled on, the truth was beginning to seep in. Clark wasn't coming home anytime soon, and I didn't want to continue feeling this way. I convinced myself that this breakup was for the best and needed to continue if I wanted to be free of him and my dependency on him and move forward.

And I did. I wanted to move forward. I wanted to restart my life. I was about to turn seventeen, and for the first time, going to college was a thought I wanted to entertain. Hearing classmates talking about which colleges they were going to and hearing stories about dorm life excited me, and it got me thinking, *Can I do what they are doing?*

All along, I had been told we couldn't afford college—and I need not even think or ask about going. I thought, *Well then, I won't ask.* Freeing myself from Clark reminded me I was in control of my life.

I set up college tours and checked into scholarships and financial aid. I arranged, set up, paid for, and took the college exams all by myself. I felt so confident in myself and my abilities that I started applying to colleges.

I was starting to feel better. I still loved and missed Clark, but my heart quit beating so fast all the time. I could finally breathe normally again. I had some friends and was doing all the high school things. I even went on a few dates. I went to my first high school party. I didn't love it; it reminded me of my parents' parties at home, except the high school kids were way less drunk.

I felt happy, and I prided myself on the fact that I felt this way as a single person and wasn't based on Clark or any other person. That was new for me.

*　　*　　*

When I woke up the weekend of my seventeenth birthday, Clark was sitting on my couch. I was shocked and let out a squeal. My heart leaped, and I could feel the smile on my face. Clark stood up, and I ran into his arms. It felt so good to have his arms around me. It felt natural for both of us; our bodies fit together like they were made for each other. We held the embrace for what seemed like forever; I didn't want to let go. I had missed that so much.

My dad walked in and said, "What is going on in here?"

Ignoring him, I stepped back from Clark and said, "What are you doing here?"

"You haven't spent a birthday without me in the last three years. Why start now?"

I love this guy. I can't believe he came all this way to see me on my birthday. I am the luckiest girl in the world! There is no one else I would prefer to spend my birthday with.

We had a great weekend; it felt like old times but a little freer. We laughed and talked. It felt so good to be beside him after six months. We didn't discuss the relationship, boundaries, or anything like that; we just enjoyed what was and left it there. Honestly, it didn't bother me; we didn't have to be an official couple to experience the love I felt between us. We were magic: I couldn't explain it, but the love was still there. Distance had not taken that from us. We might not know how to navigate a long-distance relationship, but that was okay; we knew how to pick up right where we had left off.

That weekend made me realize how much I missed Clark and how I still wanted him in my life. He was my best friend. The visit was exactly what I needed: the reassurance that we would be fine and that it was okay to proceed with my plans. Both could exist and thrive.

Life has a weird way of working itself out, I thought.

* * *

I was working and saving as much money as possible for college. I had friends and felt like I belonged. I was content with the direction of my life. I had hope for my future, which came from within me and not from anyone else. I had a goal of what I wanted and a vision of the future I intended to create. *I could be the first in my family to attend college.* That thought alone made me want to achieve it more than ever. *Won't everyone be proud of me for this? They will surely love me then.*

Thanksgiving was approaching, and Clark had called to ask if I wanted to spend it with him and his family. *Duh, of course.* "I have the flu, but I should be better before then."

"Kristie, I had a dream you were pregnant."

I giggled. "That's more like a nightmare."

"Do you think you might be?

"I don't think so."

There was no way I could be pregnant, I thought. I hadn't seen him since September. *Hmm … when was the last time I had my period? I have no idea. I stopped having my period when I lost all that weight a few months back.*

I bought three tests, and they were all negative. *Phew!* I called Clark that night and told him.

"I don't believe it. I think you're pregnant."

After school, my friend and I went by DayBreak Crisis Pregnancy Center. They gave me a pregnancy test, and it was positive. I about melted. *What in the world?*

The lady asked, "Would you like to see your baby?"

"I guess," I replied.

The next thing I saw was an alien-looking thing on a screen that was supposed to be my baby. I was in complete shock. *This is not what I was expecting. This can't be happening.*

The lady explained that I was almost ten weeks along, and everything looked perfect. She asked if I knew what I wanted to do. *How can I know what I want to do when less than five minutes ago, I didn't know this situation existed?*

She told me I had three options: keep it, give it up for adoption, or have an abortion.

Shocked and overwhelmed, I ran to the car.

My friend caught up with me and gave me an ultrasound picture. I stared at it, trying to comprehend that a baby was inside my body. *My baby!*

This is where things quickly became complicated. My vision of the future and things going well was short-lived. My life had taken a U-turn, and I suddenly had more significant decisions to make than college. Clark's surprise birthday visit turned out to be quite a bigger surprise than we could have ever imagined.

What am I going to do? What do I want to do? I kept replaying my options: adoption, abortion, or keeping it. None of them felt like much of an option, but I knew abortion wasn't my answer. I didn't like the thought of adoption, and I certainly didn't know how to raise a baby. *This is a very bad situation, Kristie.*

I knew I should tell Clark, but we weren't necessarily a couple. Just last week, we were telling each other about our dates. I didn't want to say anything until I knew what I wanted to do. I didn't want to get back together just because of a baby. I wanted him to choose me because of me—not because of a baby. *That's assuming, Kristie. What if he doesn't want this baby? What if he asks you to have an abortion?*

I will not have an abortion!

Well, there's one less option.

Does Clark even get a choice?

Yes, he does.

No, he doesn't.

Kristie, this is your decision!

Since I couldn't handle all the possibilities and scenarios running through my mind, I made an executive decision. This is my choice, and I get to make it alone.

What do I do? What do I do? What do I do?

Make a decision.

I don't know how.

You just did!

But what if it's wrong?

I knew I needed someone to talk to, but Clark was the only person I had, and he wasn't an option right now.

But God is always at work.

My teacher wrote me up for missing so many classes and sent me to the guidance counselor's office. Overwhelmed by the intensity of what was happening, I broke down and told her everything, which turned out to be a huge blessing.

She arranged for a clinical therapist to come once a week during my lunch and talk with me. This woman was sent straight from heaven above. I can't imagine what I would have done without her. Just having someone listen helped me tremendously. In the second meeting, she told me it was normal for things to feel overwhelming and complicated right now, but they wouldn't always feel like this. She said that's why it was so important to make a decision I could live with for the rest of my life—not just one that suited my life right then.

"I am seventeen years old! How can I know what I can or cannot live with the rest of my life?" I asked.

She sensed my hesitation toward abortion and told me if I thought I could never forgive myself for aborting my baby, that probably wasn't the option. She steered me toward adoption, but I couldn't imagine someone else raising *my* baby. My mom didn't want or raise me, and I had always felt like a burden to everyone. I couldn't imagine doing the same thing to *my* baby. That left me with only one option.

Right then, I committed to raising my baby. We might be poor, but I was capable of loving my baby. I just hoped that would be enough.

I called Clark. As soon as he answered the phone, I went on an entire spiel without a single breath. "Clark, I love you. You are my best friend, but I *am* pregnant, and I *am* going to have this baby. I know this complicates things, and if you don't want to be with me, don't choose to be with me because of a baby. I'll be okay, but I've got to have this baby. It's the right decision for me—with or without you."

"Kristie, slow down and breathe. It's okay."

"Clark, I have thought about this, and you can't change my mind. I cannot have an abortion; it would be the end of us. I am going to keep my baby. I don't know how, but I'll figure it out. We don't have to talk about this or make any life decisions right now."

"Kristie, slow down!"

"It's just so much, Clark."

"I knew you were pregnant. I had a feeling."

"What are we going to do?"

"I don't know, but we'll figure it out. I'll come home this weekend and talk to my parents."

I felt better after talking to him. *It's going to be okay. We're going to be alright.*

I was so scared of telling my dad that when it was just Patty and me alone at the house, I asked her how I should tell him.

She didn't ask questions. She looked at me calmly and said, "I'll handle it tonight when you go to work. Spend the night at Mamaw's, and I'll call you in the morning."

That was the entire conversation between us. I left for work, and she called me the following day to tell me I could come home after school.

Patty and I didn't talk about the situation for another few months, and my dad didn't speak to me until I brought Katelyn home from the hospital. Once, while in my presence, he said, "I knew she'd end up just like her mom." Besides that incident, he didn't look at me or acknowledge me the entire time I was pregnant. I guess that's where I got my "If you don't think about it, it's not real" delusion.

*   *   *

Attending school and working every night left me exhausted, and hardly allowed time to talk to Clark. When I got home, I didn't have the emotional energy to talk or the physical energy to stay awake. When I did speak to him, he sounded different. I felt a bad vibe coming from him, so I stepped back to see if it was me and my hormones or if something was wrong. He seemed unbothered by our one conversation a week, which confused me. I assumed we would talk a little more since we were having a baby together, but nothing had changed since I found out I was pregnant. I didn't want to push too hard, so I just let it be.

He knows how I feel; it's up to him now.

As the weeks went by, I felt myself becoming angry again: angry at the situation, mad at Clark, and upset at myself for letting this happen. I was so disappointed in myself that, I, like so many other women in my family, had gotten pregnant so young and out of marriage. Something I vowed I'd never do.

I was even more frustrated that I was having a baby with someone who I didn't even know if he was my boyfriend. We hadn't even touched that subject. We avoided it. Eventually, our one conversation a week began to feel forced and awkward. I didn't care. I was mad at him and the world. I could see my life taking a 360-degree turn from what I had planned for just a few months ago while he remained the same.

I suspected Clark had other girls around, which was worse than just a casual date. I heard their voices in the background. Of course, he said they weren't there for him.

One night, I couldn't stop crying when we got off the phone. I felt the weight of the reality of my situation for the first time. *Kristie, this may not be okay. This might not turn out alright. It usually doesn't for you anyway, why would this time be any different? I* felt so alone and unloved at that moment. Everything was becoming too much for me. *I don't have a clue. I'm barely seventeen, pregnant, still in high school, and have no one to talk to about this. Clark used to be the person I talked to about everything, but I can't talk to him because he's the problem.*

Just then, I felt my baby kick. As I was having a pity party, I felt my baby kick. It's as if she was saying, "Hello, I'm here. You aren't alone." I sobbed even more. *My sweet baby girl, you are right. You are here. I am not alone. I have you. It may just be you and me, baby girl—us against the world—but I always promise to love and protect you.*

During the last two months of my pregnancy, I quit talking to Clark. Mentally, I couldn't do it. Whenever I got off the phone with him, I was always in tears or anxious. I felt drained and defeated; it would take forever for my heart rate to go down, which delayed my sleep. I got to the point where I knew I needed to avoid that whole ordeal, so I stopped calling. It seemed so much simpler and undramatic this way. I realized I had to take care of myself to care for this baby growing inside me.

* * *

Whatever is true, whatever is noble, whatever is right, whatever
is pure, whatever is lovely, whatever is admirable—if anything
is excellent or praiseworthy—think about such things.
—Philippians 4:8

* * *

On June 7, 1995, I graduated and went into labor. A baby seemed like the appropriate graduation gift, considering I had been pregnant my entire senior year.

Clark was at my graduation and had arrived back in Nashville only a few hours before his mom called to tell him I was in labor. Even though things were strained between us, I was happy that he got to witness the birth of his child. Two days later, Katelyn and I went home to my parent's house, and Clark returned to college.

Patty and my dad immediately acted as if Katelyn belonged to them. They would tell me when to feed and bathe her, how long to hold her, when to put her down, and how long to let her cry. Everything they told me contradicted what my book or doctor told me, and when I would try to tell them, they would say I was wrong or that doctors and books were ignorant.

At first, I felt like they were trying to help, and I was patient. However, I began to see they weren't just trying to help. They wanted to be in charge. Why did that shock me? My dad was in charge of everything and everyone, and now he and Patty had something they could be in charge of together.

I didn't know how to handle the situation, which only worsened. Their rules had grown extensively with Katelyn. I couldn't drive in the rain, have her out after dark, or leave her with anyone. She felt like a Gremlin to me.

They would threaten or manipulate me if I objected or tried to do something different than what they said. Once, I had dinner with Clark's parents and didn't get home until dark. My dad locked me out of the house and told me if that ever happened again, he would call the police, and they would take Katelyn away from me.

I believed him. At seventeen, I did not know I was allowed to parent my child because I didn't think I could make my own decisions. How could I be her voice if I didn't know I had a voice? Sadly, I was too scared to ask for it or demand it.

Katelyn was twelve weeks old when Clark called to tell me he was moving back home. I was so happy to hear that. Regardless of our relationship status, he was her dad and could have a say in things that affected her. *Now if they threaten to take her or have her taken away, Clark will get her.*

That thought soothed my soul. The last thing I would ever want was for my child to be raised in the same environment I was.

> The heart is deceitful above all things and beyond
> cure. Who can understand it?
> —Jeremiah 17:9

* * *

Clark was only home three nights before we made a huge decision. I was in my bedroom, and I heard some commotion. I had just gotten Katelyn to sleep, and

I went out to ask them to be quieter—but what I found startled me. Patty and my daddy were physically fighting.

I started screaming at them to stop. What I witnessed was appalling; I had seen this before, but this was bad!

My mind was racing, *I've got to get Katelyn out of here. I've got to get Katelyn out of here.*

I tried to get her in the car seat as fast as possible, but my hands were shaking. I grabbed the diaper bag and started to walk out the door.

My dad ran in front of me to block the door. "Where do you think you are going?"

"I'm leaving."

"You're not going anywhere."

"I am not staying here! My child will not grow up the same way I did." *I cannot believe I just said that to him.*

"You can leave, but you're not taking that baby anywhere."

I screamed, "Get out of my way—or I will call the police."

He laughed an evil laugh, and I saw the look in his eyes change. He said, "I dare you," and snatched the car seat from my hands.

Something in me snapped. Maybe it was the momma bear instincts or the trauma of what I had just witnessed, but he wasn't going to manipulate me with my child any longer. *I am her mother. I belong to her, and she belongs to me.* I grabbed the phone and dialed 911. He ran over and hung up the phone on me. I grabbed the car seat and ran out the door quickly.

I made it to the end of the street and had to pull over. I cried so hard I couldn't see, and my body shook. As I sat there, I thought about what had just happened and vowed never to return. *I won't ever go back! I will not let Katelyn grow up watching this! I won't do it. I've got to do better for her. I want to do better for her. She deserves better.*

I arrived at Clark's house and started crying again as I retold the story. "I can't go back there. I can't take my baby back there, Clark! What just happened is not okay! I have to protect her. That's my job. If I go back, I will fail her."

Clark was hugging me, but my body was still shaking. "Calm down. You are safe now. Stay the night here, and we will figure out something tomorrow."

After I calmed down, we sat outside for more than two hours that night, mostly in silence. This massive weight was pressing on us; I could feel it in the air. It was bigger than anything we had ever had to figure out before. I think the reality that Clark was now responsible for more than himself must have sunk in, and after a long silence, he turned to me and said, "I guess we should get married and get a home for her then."

"Clark, I do not want you to marry me because you feel sorry for me."

"I don't feel sorry for you, but I have a responsibility to her."

"You can have a responsibility to her without marrying me."

"My parents said this was the right thing to do, and I want to do right by you and her."

I just shook my head. This wasn't what I expected or wanted, but what other choice did I have? I knew the reality was either getting married or returning to my parent's house. At least Clark would be a safer option for us.

We started making plans to get married and get our own place. We didn't discuss the condition of our relationship, what the last year had been like or done to us, or how we felt. We both pretended that space between us didn't exist because none of that mattered now. After all, we had a solution to our problem.

I saw and felt so many red flags, but I had no idea what to do about them. *Why address them now? It will only hinder things.* I told myself we would deal with that stuff later.

Right now, we have a baby who needs a safe home, and this is the best option. Besides, the past is in the past. None of that matters anymore. We'll get married, move forward, and start a new life together. We once loved each other deeply. I am sure we will find that love again. Everything will be just fine. Remember, Clark and I are magic. It will all work out. That's what I kept telling myself every time a doubt would pop up or someone would question if this was the right thing to do. *Of course, it's the right thing to do. We're thinking of our baby and not ourselves. How could that not be the right thing to do?*

So, that's just what we did. We got married on December 9, 1995, six months after I'd graduated and three months after Clark returned home from college.

> *Everything will be just fine. It will all work out.* That's what I kept telling myself every time a doubt would pop up or someone would question if this was the right thing to do.

* * *

My dad wasn't thrilled about me getting married, and his participation and budget were minimal. He said, "You want me to waste my money on something I think is ridiculous and won't last?"

I shrugged. "I'm getting married whether you help me or not."

"I'll give you a thousand dollars. Don't ask for more—and I want my money back when you get a divorce."

"Deal."

"Don't be thinking you have my blessing because you don't."

I giggled. Of course, I didn't, but I didn't care. I had a wedding to plan. The only thing I knew about a wedding was the dress. I had always envisioned a Cinderella-style wedding dress. Of course, I envisioned the prince, the castle, and the fireworks accompanying it.

Boy, was I wrong. In so many ways!

I would soon learn that a thousand dollars wouldn't get me far. This was the start of my thriftiness. I sprang into action. I found a cake lady who worked out of her home, and a friend of a friend did the catering. We used Clark's parents' church, and my mom offered to do my flowers. I did my own hair and makeup.

And my dress? I happened to be in the mall in a store called JB White's. I didn't know they sold wedding dresses. I walked quickly, trying to get out the door because Katelyn was screaming when the dress caught my eye. There were only two dresses left. The store was going out of business, and the dress was 90 percent off the original price. I asked the lady if she would hold it for me to come back and try it on. I had a screaming baby and no money with me.

The clerk said, "No holds and no returns."

I put the dress back on the rack.

As I walked away, an elderly lady caught up and said, "That dress would look beautiful on you."

I explained the situation to her and shyly said, "It'll be okay, but thank you."

"What if I lend you the money?"

"Oh, no, ma'am, you can't do that. It's okay."

"Yes, come back here. Let's get the dress, and you can mail me a check. Besides, you can't walk away from a ninety-dollar wedding dress."

"I don't even know if it will fit."

"Sweet girl, there's only one way to find out, and besides, you could have it altered."

I didn't know what to do—Katelyn was really screaming—but I said okay and left with a dress.

So, there you go. I went wedding dress shopping with a stranger, and the dress fit perfectly. (And, in case you're wondering, I did mail her a check!)

*   *   *

The anticipated day finally arrived. I had spent three months planning and stressing over that day. Many people were at my house, and it was time to go to the church. I could hear everyone outside the bathroom asking where I was.

I could hear them calling my name, yet I remained quiet, locked inside the bathroom, wondering if I would come out.

I was crippled with fear. I kept thinking, *I cannot let my dad be right about this, but what if he is? Am I doing the right thing? Does Clark really love me? Do I really love him? The rest of our lives!*

I'm not gonna cry.

I'm not gonna cry.

I'm not gonna cry!

I cannot cry. It will ruin my makeup.

Deep breaths.

Inhale.

Exhale.

I can just run away if I can clear the house and reach my car.

Wait, I have to get Katelyn.

Who has Katelyn? Who did I see holding Katelyn?

I could grab her, pretend I am going to the church, but keep driving.

Where would I go?

Where would I stay?

I don't have much money.

Maybe my aunt in Kentucky?

I don't know what to do. I don't know what to do. I don't know what to do.

What do I do?

Breathe. Breathe. Breathe.

You've got to pull yourself together. You can do this.

You are getting married today, baby girl. Chin up.

Yes, I'm getting married today!

My heart is beating out of my chest. My face and neck are on fire. I'm starting to stink from sweating so badly.

I love Clark, but does he love me? Does he truly love me? What if he's only marrying me because it's the right thing to do?

We haven't been together for the past year—and now we're getting married?

This is absurd!

We need to wait.

We need more time.

We need to make sure this is what we really want to do.

But you can't live here.

You need to get out.

You don't want to keep Katelyn in this house.

We have to get married. It's the right thing to do.

Clark loves you. You're just overreacting.

What if I don't love him?
You do love him. You're just afraid he doesn't love you.
But do I love Clark?
Get up, unlock the door, and drive to the church.
And quit talking to yourself.

My thoughts were interrupted by a loud bang on the door, "Open this door! Open this door right now and get out here! Kristie! You are going to this wedding! I have paid too much money for you not to come out of this bathroom. You have two minutes to get out here—or I will bust the door down and get you myself."

And then I quickly remembered why I wanted to get married.

My marriage started with me convincing myself that I had cold feet, everyone else had cold feet, and it would all be fine. Marrying Clark was "the right thing to do." Once we were married, everything would be amazing and beautiful—just as I had always dreamed. I knew I was marrying Clark because I thought it was the right thing to do for Katelyn, and I wanted to get out of that house. I knew Clark was marrying me because his parents raised him to be a good man and to take care of his responsibilities, and that's what Katelyn and I were: a responsibility.

Don't get me wrong. I loved Clark, and I knew Clark loved me. I just wondered if we were getting married for the right reason.

Regardless, I made it to that church and vowed to love and honor Clark. And I intended to do that.

I just didn't know how hard it would be.

CHAPTER 3

THE START OF A DISASTROUS DECADE

We went skiing on our honeymoon, which I had never done, and I was terrible! But just being with Clark for an entire week felt magical. Being with your best friend twenty-four hours a day, seven days a week, sounded like a dream. I longed to be around people I loved and who loved me in return.

But the honeymoon wasn't like I'd imagined. I truly did not learn how to ski. After a two-hour glacial trek down the mountain—an absolute disaster, despite all Clark's attempts to teach me—I told him to ski if he wanted to, but I'd be in the condo for my safety and the safety of everyone on the mountain.

So for the next three days of our "honeymoon," I sat in the condo while Clark skied (since we'd paid for the lift tickets, he used them). I felt sad and disappointed. Wasn't I worth more than a lift ticket? Wasn't spending time "together" the point of a honeymoon? I kept thinking, *Clark got stuck with me.* I had hoped that getting married and going on a honeymoon would change things and that we would pick up where we had left off. We used to be so good at that.

By the fifth day, I had to admit that the magical honeymoon wasn't happening. I finally told Clark how I felt, and he stopped skiing and spent the next two days with me. Unfortunately, the magic couldn't be revived.

Clark and I walked through this dreamy, snowy town that looked like something out of a Hallmark movie, but it didn't feel like a Hallmark movie. It felt stuffy and forced. I felt the enormous gap between us and thought this might have been a mistake.

I didn't want to feel like that, plus I wasn't ready to accept defeat so early, so I convinced myself that things weren't as bad as I thought. *Things will look up once we get home to our daughter. We have a lifetime together, and Katelyn, Clark, and I will finally become a real family. Indeed, the magic will start then.* I adopted this belief and held onto it for several years because I wanted it to be true. If only my hope had been enough for us.

The honeymoon, unfortunately, was a sign of how marriage was going to go: basically, not at all, according to my expectations. A few months after getting married, the reality of assuming all my financial responsibilities and a baby led Clark to get a second job: a second shift in addition to his third-shift job. We only saw him for about an hour a day, but he was usually so tired that he wanted to rest or watch TV.

I expected this season would be hard and knew we wouldn't see each other a lot, but I imagined the time we did have together would be better than it was. However, it wasn't just his work schedule that kept us apart; he started going out with his friends on an occasional Friday night. I didn't like it, but I kept telling myself, *It won't* be *like this forever. Everything will work out. Give it some time.* I convinced myself that all newlyweds go through this; we were just a little different because we had a baby, and he worked third shift.

Deep down, I felt guilty that Clark had gotten stuck with me because I got pregnant. I knew it was my fault he had to work so much that I could continue school and be home with Katelyn. I was grateful for how he provided for us. I didn't complain, even though I was crushed inside. The changes started slowly, but isn't that how most bad habits or sins start? Slowly but continuously. It's such a slow fade that you can miss it, or if you do see it, you might make excuses for it if you're not ready to confront it. I know I did. I tried to justify it to put my mind at ease. *He's just nineteen, Kristie. Give him a break. He deserves it. Let him have some fun. He works hard for you. It won't be this way forever.*

The occasional Friday night out with his friends became every Friday night, and home by ten turned into midnight. Drinking a little quickly turned into drinking a lot.

At first, I tried talking to him about it, but that went in one ear and out the other. He acted like he understood and would apologize. He would say he wouldn't do it again, but he would do it again the following weekend. He would lie and say he got home at a decent hour even though I knew better because I was awake. I would tell him he was lying, and he would swear he wasn't.

I started waiting up for him to prove when he got home, and I wanted to see what condition he came home in. The condition was hardly ever sober. This was a bad idea. Seeing him like this reminded me of my dad and the life I vowed never to live. Rage would take over me because he acted as if this were no big deal, and I knew full well this could be starting a lifelong pattern. His nonchalant attitude toward me, and my anger toward him, resulted in long, heated arguments.

My heart was breaking watching him live this life, but he didn't see the problem. I was the problem in his mind because I was griping and complaining. This wasn't the Clark I used to know. He had changed so much in two years that I hardly recognized him.

I would say things were spiraling out of control, but they were never under control. We had never established boundaries or expectations or had conversations about our hopes and dreams for ourselves or our family. We had never expressed a direction we wanted our marriage to go. We didn't have marriage counseling or a wise person to offer advice. We were two naïve nineteen-year-olds with a baby, trying to play house without a clue.

Going into my marriage, I only wanted to make Clark happy. I thought if I made him happy, he would love me, and if he loved me, that would make me happy. Wasn't the goal for both of us to be happy?

It didn't take long to realize that earning love in my marriage would be just as hard as earning it with everyone else. *Once again, I'm doing everything I think someone wants me to do, things that should make them happy, and it's not working. I don't feel loved. I don't feel wanted. I don't feel important. I guess I thought it would be easier being married, and I thought Clark would make me feel all those things, especially if I'm doing all the things I'm supposed to.*

I knew the drill: try harder. I did, but not much changed except he stayed gone more. And the less I saw him, the unhappier I felt. I already didn't feel chosen, and his being gone all the time didn't help my feelings. They only grew worse.

* * *

Our first anniversary came, and I assumed we would celebrate and eat the cake that had been in our freezer for a year, but I was wrong. Clark decided to go out with the boys that night, but he forgot to tell me. I sat home alone; our anniversary night was no different than any other Friday night to him.

I tried to make sense of it all. *Why would he not come home on our anniversary? Why would he not call? Does he even know it's our anniversary? Of course, he does. Clark is better than this. What is going on with him?* In my mind, I was trying to think of all the reasons he was not here: his truck broke down, he's stuck in traffic, he got busy at work. *It's ten o'clock, Kristie. He would have been home by now if any of those things had happened.*

The longer I sat there in my head, the angrier I got.

Clark will be home anytime now. Be patient.

I know I've been making excuses for him because I don't want to accept or admit any other possibility. *It's nothing, Kristie. Don't think like that. We won't become my parents; we just won't.*

Surely, Clark would not do this to us on our anniversary.

Oh, but he is.

I wanted to get up and smash that cake, but it kept staring at me. I went to throw it in the trash, but I couldn't bring myself to do it. Instead, I took a bite and started to cry. Eating the cake alone just felt wrong. *Is this really what marriage looks like? I had more faith in us than this.*

He has left you home alone on your anniversary without so much as a phone call.

But this is not the Clark I know.

Oh, but it is.

My heart hurt, and I felt like I was starting to lose hope. When I walked down that aisle, I committed to putting our past behind us, entering with a clean slate, and doing everything it took to make this marriage work. And I had been.

Maybe you made that commitment alone. You are eating your cake alone.

That was the first time I ever felt alone in this marriage. I don't know why since I was always alone. I spent five nights alone because of his job, and now I spent six because of his friends. I was starting to feel like his friends were more important than me. *His friends are more important than you, Kristie. Can't you see that? If he wanted to be home with you, he would be here.*

The truth was obvious: I was not important enough for him to come home to. I was his wife, and he didn't want me. *He got stuck with you, Kristie, just like Patty got stuck with you.*

Clark could have walked away, but he didn't. Doesn't that mean something?

Patty could have walked away, and I understood the same to be true in this situation.

Even if Clark got stuck with me, things could still turn out well, like with Patty, if I worked hard enough.

Since Clark had chosen to marry me, I needed to be grateful.

I liked this way of thinking because it protected me from reality. This way of thinking told me we would be okay. Suddenly, I didn't feel so sad for myself anymore. Instead, I felt sorry for him. After all, he was trying to do the right thing.

That night I chose to be grateful. I quit nagging and complaining. I stopped waiting up for him, and the nasty arguments ceased. I started trying to figure out who he wanted me to be so I could become her. *If I become her, he will like it and stay home more.*

It was hard to figure out because he was never home, and we barely spoke. *Remember what you learned from childhood? You have to please him in order to be loved. Try that, Kristie, and try harder.*

So, that's what I tried to do in my marriage: make Clark's life as easy as possible. I wouldn't ask him to do anything around the house if he had to work so hard and so much outside the home.

Since I didn't want him to become stressed or feel weighed down because me or Katelyn, I let him do whatever he wished. He came and went as he pleased. He spent his weekends however he chose. I did not want to inconvenience him, so I didn't ask him for help of any kind. Asking for help would make me a needy and high-maintenance wife. I wanted to be easy and compliant, so he would be happy and choose me. I did everything I thought I should to make his life as easy as possible, thinking this would make him happy in return. I would clean and try to cook, even though I didn't have a clue about cooking. Maybe one day he wouldn't consider himself stuck with me; maybe he would even be happy with me. We were happy before he left for college. If I am good enough, maybe we can be happy again.

I wish I could tell you that it worked, and we lived happily ever after, but if that were the case, this would be the end of the book, and clearly, this is just the beginning. The truth was that Clark just wasn't interested in me or the life I had to offer, and giving him total freedom without consequences (nagging, complaining, or screaming) only created a monster.

Eventually, Clark coming home at midnight turned into whenever the bars closed. And Friday nights turned into Saturday nights as well.

Maybe I really was just unworthy of love. Maybe I really was just unlovable. Maybe I wasn't even really wanted? This fear was about to be confirmed.

*   *   *

Wake up, sleeper, rise from the dead, and Christ will shine on you.
—Ephesians 5:14

*   *   *

One night, Clark came home drunk without his wedding ring. This particular night was the only night I remember ever asking him to stay home. We had our second child, Kelsey, a few weeks prior, and I was sleep deprived and desperately hoping for some help. Clark didn't necessarily say no; instead, he made me a deal. He promised to stay home for an entire month if he could go out that night. *A whole month? I could hardly wait!*

Up until that point, I was very naive about what exactly took place when he went out. I knew he drank a little, oftentimes a little too much, but I never thought he was looking for girls. I really don't know what I thought was going on. His friends were single, so I don't understand why this had never occurred to me. Denial maybe? Naïveté? In my nineteen-year-old brain, married people didn't do this. Well, I knew they did, but I believed Clark and I were different.

Looking back, I ignored all the signs because I didn't want to deal with the truth. The truth may have held me accountable or forced me to make decisions I wasn't ready to make. *We have two children together, and he would never do anything to mess that up. He's just having a little fun. He works so hard; he deserves it.*

I ignored it because I was lonely, sad, and empty. I thought I had found my safe space with Clark, and he would provide the acceptance, longing, and love I had been looking for, which I had spent a lifetime craving.

But here we are, and the evidence is right before me. I can't deny it any longer. I must admit the truth. I felt sad, confused, angry, and hurt … but what do I do? I love him and don't want our family to split up. *Why would he do this? Is he not happy? What is he lacking at home? What am I not doing right?*

Your marriage is out of control, Kristie, if you can even call it that. When are you going to wake up?

Standing there looking at him, with him being in no shape to give me answers, left me teetering between the reality of what had happened and the possibility that it was my fault.

Deep down, in the back of my mind, I had failed him. In the past two and a half years, I hadn't been able to earn his love, and it was somehow my fault that I wasn't good enough or fun enough to make him want to stay home. So, instead of being angry at him, I was mad at myself for not being able to provide the home that he needed or wanted.

The following day, I was so angry at him—and I was sad at the same time. I couldn't decide whether to help him or punch him in the face. He felt terrible, physically and emotionally. I wanted to help him, but I could barely look at him. I was ashamed of him and angry at myself for allowing things to get this far. However, he didn't even know what had happened or what he had done. He kept asking me why he felt so bad and why I was being mean to him. I explained to him what had transpired, and he looked so confused.

He had no recollection of what had happened. He said he was sorry and promised that it would never happen again.

"So … you're telling me someone slipped something in your drink and took off your wedding ring? Why would they do that?"

"I don't know, but I didn't take off my wedding ring. I'll admit I had too much to drink, but I did not take off my ring … I swear."

Don't buy it, Kristie. Do not believe that story. That story doesn't make sense. Girls wouldn't do that to guys … maybe if it were the other way around.

I wanted to believe him. He had never done this before, so he deserved to have me believe him, right? I had to believe him; it wouldn't be right if I didn't.

He was looking for another girl, Kristie. This is not okay. Do you want your girls growing up watching this?

He promised he would never do it again.

The wedding ring incident was just the beginning of a long toxic cycle of our marriage.

Clark would do something wrong, and I would get mad and complain. He would feel bad and try to make it up to me. I would relish and enjoy the extra attention and play off of it for as long as I could. Hey, negative attention is still attention!

Sadly, though, these were the only times I felt loved by him. The only time he ever consciously showed me attention. And the sad part is they were lies. That's not real or true love—that was Clark trying to get out of trouble—but I didn't know any better. Those were the same lies I had watched growing up; they were lies I believed; they were lies that made me feel loved; they were lies that made me feel validated; and they were lies that I would not have traded (at the time) even for the truth because the truth hurt worse than the lies.

And, so, I let it continue.

But day after day, month after month, the anger and resentment growing inside of me started seeping out. Eventually, it became a regular part of me. I started waiting up for him again, which resulted in heated arguments and screaming matches every time he got home late or didn't show up when or where he was supposed to.

He would dismiss my concerns and tell me how ridiculous I was to be thinking the things I accused him of doing. He told me he deserved time to be a man because he worked hard and gave all his money to us. Before long, we were slaying each other without remorse, and this started to scare me because neither of us was backing down. It became painfully obvious that my home was beginning to look a lot like my childhood, minus the physical abuse.

Clark would say, "If you don't like me going out alone, then come with me." But I wouldn't, and he knew that. I grew up watching that my whole life and vowed never to do that to my kids.

This kept me in constant conflict between my head and heart. I believed it was my fault that he had to go out without me. But I still couldn't understand why he wouldn't stay home or do things with us—or maybe even he and I go out alone. Was that asking for too much? I didn't think so, but every time I asked, he had an excuse.

So I complained, and he reminded me that I was invited, so I couldn't complain. So I didn't—until I did.

Clark continued to pursue his hobbies, his drinking, and his friends for the next two years after the ring incident, but somehow, he was around long enough for me to get pregnant again.

Making up really is fun to do. I loved being a mom, and one more excited me; that was just one more to love. In my distorted, messed up way of thinking, I thought, *Maybe this one will be the one that will somehow make Clark realize we need him and want him, and he will finally choose us.*

The vicious cycle kept spinning, though, and with each passing episode, the momentum picked up. Every time I thought things couldn't get any worse, they did.

*   *   *

Everyone should be quick to listen, slow to speak and slow to become angry, because human anger does not produce the righteousness that God desires.
—James 1:19–20

*   *   *

It was Christmas Eve, and I was at the mall for some last-minute things. I ran into a guy who worked with Clark, and he was with his wife. We stopped and said the obligatory "How are you?" and "Merry Christmas."

I casually said, "Must be nice to get off early. Clark has to work all day."

The wife looked at her husband as if she was allowing him the opportunity to speak, but he didn't. She said, "Kristie, I just pulled this one from the strip club—and Clark was there."

"Are you sure it was Clark?" I asked. *Surely, Clark wasn't there. That didn't make sense. Clark likes to drink and go out with the boys … but a strip club at two o'clock in the afternoon on Christmas Eve? No way!*

"Oh, yes, it was Clark," she said.

As if I needed confirmation, I looked at the husband—who looked mortified that his wife was spilling his business—and said, "Was Clark at the club with you?"

He didn't actually answer the question; he just nodded.

I stormed out of the mall. *There has to be a reasonable explanation for this, and I'm going to find out what it is.*

Clark wasn't home when I got there and wouldn't answer his cell phone. Something told me to go ahead and take the girls to my parents so they wouldn't be there when he got home.

When Clark finally got home, he said, "Hey," and he headed straight to the shower as if nothing were different than any other day.

I asked, "Where have you been?"

"We got off a little early, and I went for a quick drink with some guys."

"It's Christmas Eve. Why wouldn't you come home to be with us if you got off early?"

"Jim took us out for a drink. His treat."

"But it's Christmas Eve. And why couldn't you have called and told me?"

"It was just a quick drink!"

He got into the shower, and I left the bathroom.

There is something more to this story, Kristie.

I passed by his phone and immediately checked it. It felt wrong, but I wanted to calm my nerves to see if I was overreacting. I picked it up and hit redial. (This was 1999, and we didn't have fancy cell phones like we do today. Redial was my only option.)

"Hello?" a female voice answered.

"Um ... who is this?"

Click.

I called again. No answer. Again. No answer. Again. No answer.

I left a message. I'm not even sure what I said.

I could hear Clark go from the bathroom to the bedroom to outside and then back and forth. I knew he was looking for his phone. He went out to his truck, and I could see the panic in his behavior. Finally, after a few more minutes of searching, I called out, "Looking for this?"

Casually, he said, "Yes."

I don't know why I said what I said. I didn't even realize what I said until it came out of my mouth: "Your girlfriend called."

His eyes got huge, and I knew right then. He didn't have to say a word. Instead of reacting to what my heart knew, I said louder, "Your girlfriend called!" I wanted to be mad instead of sad.

He just stood there staring at me like a deer in headlights.

In that split second, rage filled my body, and he said nothing. I yelled in both anger and disappointment, "How could you?"

He grabbed his phone out of my hands and walked out the door.

I ran behind him, hollering, "Where are you going?"

He didn't respond.

"Clark, where are you going?" My anger was turning into panic.

"Why does it matter?"

"Because we are married, and it's Christmas Eve, and our children are waiting on us to open presents."

He got in his truck, and I pulled open the door.

He closed it again and locked it.

"Open the door!" I screamed. "Get out!"

He wouldn't answer. He started to drive away.

I held the door and screamed, "Don't leave, Clark. Please don't leave. We can fix this. I will do better. I'll quit complaining and nagging you. I'll be better. We can fix this, Clark. Please don't leave me."

He drove away, and as he did, my hand was pulled from the door, causing me to fall. His truck was out of sight before I could even look up. I was on the ground, crying, unaware of what was happening around me.

Once inside, everything felt surreal. It's like time wasn't even moving. I paced back and forth, back and forth. Somehow, I did the dishes as if my world wasn't completely falling apart. I called Clark's aunt and told her what had happened. If anyone could call him and talk some sense into him, it would be her. Instead, she told me to let him be right now and to be with my kids, so I did.

I walked in, and the first thing the girls said was, "Where's Daddy?"

"Daddy will be here soon." I didn't have the heart to tell them he wasn't coming.

They showed me their gifts, and I gave everything I had to smile and go through the motions. *Don't let them see you cry, Kristie. Don't project your feelings onto them. Allow them to have a good Christmas. Don't steal that from them.*

My insides hurt physically, and all I could think about was that he wasn't coming back this time.

The girls fell asleep, and I left them there for the night.

I went home and climbed into bed; my mind was viciously replaying everything that had transpired in the past few hours. It felt like there was a thousand-pound weight on my chest. I tried to breathe slowly, in and out. My head had difficulty comprehending what had just happened, but my body must have believed it because it wouldn't quit shaking. *My poor girls don't deserve this.*

All of a sudden, it became so clear. *Kristie, you are not worthy of Clark's sacrifices. You aren't enough. You do not matter. No matter what you do or don't do, he doesn't want you or this life. He didn't choose you; he got stuck with you. You are not important enough to him for him to give up the life he wants. You are not enough, and you will never be enough. Why can't you accept it? Stop trying, Kristie. Stop trying. You're making it worse for yourself.*

My heart felt like it had been ripped out of my chest, but finally admitting what I had known all along helped lower my heart rate. I could breathe a little easier. The truth is like ripping off a bandaid; it hurts but never as bad as you imagined.

During the night, I awoke to the sound of Clark's voice. As I walked toward the den, I heard another male voice. From the conversation, I could tell he was with that guy tonight, and one of them wrecked their car. They were scared and decided to return to our house.

Whatever, I thought. *Clark's not here for me. He's only here because he has nowhere else to go.* I heard enough, and went back to bed.

The next morning, I woke to him stirring in our bathroom. As I went to get up, my body physically hurt. Suddenly, I remembered yesterday's events and could feel my stomach turning.

Clark was shaving like he didn't have a care in the world.

Maybe he doesn't care. Maybe you're the only one with all the cares.

His being so close to me made me feel exposed and vulnerable. I felt like I should hide. I couldn't make eye contact with him. I felt too embarrassed that I had begged him to stay.

No, I felt like he should be the one hiding. He should be hiding from embarrassment and the shame of his actions, but he was standing there like he hadn't done anything wrong. *Does any of this even bother him? Even if he doesn't love me, is he not sorry about what he is doing to our kids and family?*

"Call your parents and tell them to have the girls ready so we can go to Nanny's," he hollered from the bathroom.

"You are not taking the girls away from me for the next three days."

"Then I suggest you get ready too."

"I'm not going anywhere with you."

"I'm taking the girls so they can open their gifts. You can call your parents—or I will."

I was in awe of the words coming out of Clark's mouth. He had never taken the initiative to do anything with the girls. *This is a power move, Kristie. He only wants them because he doesn't want to tell his parents he's a liar, a cheater, and a drunk! Coward.*

✦　✦　✦

We ignored and avoided each other for the duration of the holidays. We showed up where we were expected and went through the motions. I felt like a zombie walking through the days. I watched him playing with the girls and talking to everyone as if his world was fine, and maybe it was. Perhaps it was just mine that was in complete ruins.

One night, I couldn't take the tension anymore. I was so nervous that I started crying before I even spoke. "What is going to happen to us?"

"I don't know."

"You don't know? What do you mean you don't know?" Sadness and rage flowed through my body. "You do this to our family and don't know what will happen? Did you not stop to think about what it would look like when you ripped our family apart?" Sobbing, I held my head down and quietly said, "I think you should leave. The girls and I should get to stay in the house. This is their home, and they shouldn't have to leave because you don't want to be a part of our family."

I didn't mean it. I didn't want him to leave … or to stay.

"I will leave if you really want me to."

If I really want him to? Those words struck a nerve! "You were with another girl five nights ago; why would I not want you to?"

"I wasn't with her like you think, Kristie."

"Oh, right, Clark. Now you want me to believe this story just like I believed your wedding ring story. Just leave, Clark. Spare me the lies—and leave."

I still didn't want him to leave. I wanted him to hurt the way I hurt—even though I didn't think it was possible. He didn't care about me. He wouldn't have left me on the ground like an animal if he did. No matter how much I didn't want him to go, there wouldn't be any begging today.

"You have every reason to want me to leave, and I don't blame you. I have been a horrible husband and dad. I don't know why I haven't seen this until now. Watching you beg me to stay after what you knew I had done almost killed me. I left because I felt so much shame. I was too cowardly to stay here and face you. I will never be able to unsee the look on your face when I pulled out of the driveway. I prayed and asked God to help me fix this. I know he allowed the wreck to open my eyes, and it has. I am so sorry, Kristie. I hope it's not too late to fix our marriage?"

I felt my insides getting mushy and feared I would start crying again. *Crying is weak, Kristie. You were weak a few days ago, and you see how that turned out. Don't make that mistake again. Besides, you didn't break your marriage—Clark did.*

"Clark, you haven't once said you want to stay because you love me. I don't think you are sorry for what you did. I think you are sorry you got caught."

"Kristie, I am sorry for what I have done, what I've been doing, and how I've acted. I am so mad at myself. I knew it wasn't right, but you didn't pay me any attention. You only care about the kids. You never want to do anything with me. I'm just a paycheck to you, and you still gripe and complain about everything I do. And you constantly remind me of everything I don't do. Nothing I do could ever make you happy or be enough."

"Oh, so this is all my fault? You cheat on me, and you're the victim?"

"I'm not saying it's your fault. I'm just saying that is how I feel."

"You are a grown man who can care for himself; these girls can't. They depend on me; they need me. You don't need me—much less want me. And I only griped and complained because I wanted things to be different. I wanted you to stay home and spend time with us, instead of leaving us every weekend.

"I griped and complained because you are doing things married men shouldn't do. My griping and complaining were because I still had hope in our marriage even after you came home from the club without your wedding ring—even though I should've known better. My griping and complaining were hopeful that you would hear me and stop one day."

Quietly, he said, "I know."

I was on a roll, "You say nothing you do would be enough or make me happy! How do you even know that? You are never around long enough to try to make me happy, and you don't do anything because I do everything. And you want to know why I do it all? So you don't leave."

"I try not to ask for much. I try not to ask for your help. I try to make life easy and simple for you when you get home. I try not to complain, but you keep messing up."

"I try to be available to you and your needs, but you are never home. I don't ask you to stay home with us, but I always hope you will. I don't ask you to attend church with us, but I wish you would. I don't ask you to do anything with the girls, but you are their dad—and you should."

"I don't ask for your help because I don't want to inconvenience you or make you think we are too much of a burden. So I do it all on my own. And it is a lot! And I was afraid if you knew how much it was, you would leave us because you couldn't handle it. I have always been afraid that what just happened would happen if I asked too much of you. So I didn't, and it happened anyway."

We both got quiet for a few minutes.

I saw a tear roll down his eye and thought he might be sorry. I'd never seen a tear before, but it was too late for apologies. The damage was done. I wouldn't accept his apology if he couldn't take back my broken heart.

"You've never acted like you wanted or needed me around. And when I try to do something for the girls, I never do it right. You act like I don't know how to care for my own kids. And I always feel like I'm intruding on y'all's schedule."

"I do want you around. I have always wanted you around, Clark, but I quit begging you to stay home a year ago. It was not because I didn't want you home with us; it was because it hurt worse to hear you say no than not to ask."

"Kristie, I am sorry for what I've done, but I'm not sorry I got caught. I'm tired of how this marriage operates. Something needs to change."

"Ha ha ha. Are you tired of how it operates? Get in line, buddy."

"What's that supposed to mean," he asked.

"How can you be tired of something that constantly benefits you?"

"You act like I don't do anything. I bust my butt so you can have this life."

"And it's a great one, babe."

"Is it? You sure don't act like you appreciate it."

"Clark, you leave to go to the gym before we get up when you could help me with the girls. Should I appreciate that? You go out every weekend without us. Should I appreciate that? You stay late after work, doing who knows what ... well, never mind, now we know what, but still, should I appreciate that?" Exhausted and feeling as if no fight was left in me, I said, "Can I ask you a question?"

He nodded.

"Do you ever stop to think about me when you're out at the clubs? What I'm doing? How I'm feeling? How's my day been? Am I okay? What about the girls? Do you think about them?"

I looked over, and our eyes met. He was crying, which infuriated me for some reason.

I snapped, "Why are you crying? You don't get to cheat on me and cry about it!"

Before I finished saying those words, he was coming toward me with his arms out as if he were going to hug me.

I drew back. "I do not want the same arms around me that have been around another girl."

"You can't forgive me, can you?"

"I want to," I said softly. "I thought I could, but I don't know how. When I look at you, all I feel is disgust."

"I can tell ... the look in your eyes is different now. You have so much hatred and sadness, and I know I caused it."

"I do hate you a little bit. And I hate myself because I still love you too." I started to cry again. Saying that out loud reminded me I did still love him. *How do you make yourself stop loving someone? Do I want to stop loving him? I don't even know. I don't think so. I have loved Clark for almost half my life. Loving him somehow still brings peace to my soul—even though it torments me too. How bizarre.*

For a few minutes, we both sat there, lost in thought.

He said, "Do you want me to leave tonight?"

I shook my head. "Sleep on the couch."

As he got up to leave, I said, "Clark, is this marriage worth salvaging?"

"I hope so."

* * *

The following day, I awoke to the sounds of Clark and the kids in the kitchen. I sat there and listened for a minute. The girls were giggling, and Clark was talking to them. *What a beautiful sound,* I thought. *If only this were real instead of Clark trying to get out of trouble again. I've watched this scene play out too many times, and it never lasts.* Suddenly, it didn't sound so beautiful to me; it sounded repulsive.

I rolled over to get out of bed, and there was a note:

Kristie,

The first time I saw you, I thought you were so beautiful. I also thought, *this girl is a wild one; she's going to be trouble.* You were so sassy and confident in yourself, all the boys liked you, but you paid attention to me. I never understood why; I always felt so undeserving. The more I got to know you, I fell in love with your heart.

Kristie, you are the kindest, most unselfish person I know. You always have been, but I don't know how to be like that, that unselfish. I don't know how to give up my life for someone else like you have for the kids. I know it has been unfair to you to expect that you do everything alone, to carry the weight of our family and home all on your own. I didn't understand that burden or the weight of it all on you until last night. I don't know how I missed it other than being selfish and foolish, and I am so, so sorry for that.

Kristie, I don't like the man I've become, but I'm ready to change into the man you need. I want to change for you and our kids. We have two babies already and two more coming; it's time for me to grow up and learn how to be the man I am supposed to be. I'm willing to face my wrongs and make them right. Kristie, I love you, and it kills me that you don't think I do. My loving you has never been the issue. Ignorance, maybe, but if you give us another chance, you won't regret it. I promise I won't ever go to another club or bar as long as I live. I promise to stay home with you and the kids. I promise to be your friend, the way we used to be. I promise to devote my entire life to you right now, as I should have long ago.

Please think about it; I know I don't deserve it, but I'll spend the rest of my life making it up to you and our kids if you allow me to.

Love,
Clark

* * *

That was such a complicated conversation to have. Unexpectedly, though, I felt optimistic about our talk. We had never had a conversation like that before; it felt authentic and gave me hope. We told each other things we had never spoken of before and shared our hurts and feelings.

We discussed how I needed him to be more involved with the girls and needed him as my helpmate. I also wanted my best friend back: the Clark who loved me, talked to me, spent time with me, and did things for me and with me.

We identified that he needed intimacy to feel connected to me, to feel wanted, and to feel loved by me, and I needed communication to feel connected to him. When I didn't get communication, I withheld intimacy. When he didn't get intimacy, he withheld communication. It was a vicious cycle.

Listening to everything I did wrong reaffirmed that I had also failed him. I could see why he felt unloved and unvalued. *If he wants to try to make this work again, we should.*

What about all those promises he made? You know they will be hard to keep—maybe even impossible.

I should at least allow him the opportunity to try.

During our conversation, I heard Clark choosing our family and picking me for the first time in a very long time. That's all my heart needed to hear; it told me everything would be okay now—and I believed it. I was excited to give us a chance, a new beginning.

However, all that was on the surface level. At the deeper inside level, I still felt broken and sad. (We didn't discuss the other girl or his feelings about that.) It did occur to me once, and I thought, *He cheats on me, and I'm excited to have another chance to do better, to make things right?*

What on earth? If only I could have seen this as a sign that we were in serious trouble—I was in serious trouble.

*   *   *

The Lord is close to the brokenhearted and saves
those who are crushed in spirit.
— Psalm 34:18

PART

II

DECONSTRUCTING

CHAPTER 4

DOING WHAT WE
THOUGHT WE SHOULD

At any rate, things changed … for about twelve weeks. On the surface, we were doing well. Both of us were trying hard to make our marriage work. Clark did keep his promise, and he stopped going to the bars and clubs. He got a first-shift job and was able to quit his second job, which helped tremendously.

Clark was home more than ever. It felt so good to have him there. He was learning to do hair, homework, bath time, and night routines. I incorporated him into our lives to make him aware of daily activities and included him. I communicated with him more to show him I loved and appreciated him, but we still had difficulty connecting emotionally. I brought it up once, but since Clark said he thought things were fine, I didn't pursue it further. I thought things were better, but we were far from fine. I didn't dare voice that; I feared it might set us back.

Kristie, you might be the problem since you're the one who feels the disconnect. Just give it time.

Watching Clark with the girls and seeing him stay home definitely helped. It showed me he was serious about our marriage and family and made me believe he was genuinely sorry for what he did. However, the lack of emotional connection bothered me. Loving him felt so hard. He swore it was just me and said he didn't feel the disconnect, but he seemed to be having as much difficulty loving me as I did him.

I am still hurting; I know that much is true. Maybe that's the reason I have all these feelings. Some days, I can't get the thought out of my head that he has had an affair. He tells me it was only emotional, but I feel so betrayed. And even if it were emotional, that hurts even worse because that's the part of him I can't seem to reach.

What was she to him that I'm not? Ugh, I still feel broken and empty, but I'm holding on for all of us.

Someone told me I needed to process the hurt, talk about how it made me feel, and acknowledge that Clark caused me pain and that it still hurts. *Nah, that might rock the boat. I know he's sorry; I can see it in his changes. I am learning how to stuff the hurt, add layers, and keep busy. It works except for when it doesn't.*

I also feel numb; maybe that's the problem. How do I un-numb myself? I'm hoping that if I keep piling on enough layers, I will eventually forget about the bottom layer, which hurts the worst.

Beneath all this pain, I'm also, weirdly, optimistic. When I see the changes and watch him with the girls, I momentarily forget about my pain. I can glimpse a better future. If we keep pressing forward together, one day, we can both be whole and happy. I try to stay positive.

* * *

For three months, real change happened. We started operating like a real family. Clark came home after work, and we had dinner, played with the kids, and tag-teamed bedtime and bath time. It felt weird having him there, but I loved it. Attaining the physical parts of our marriage seemed much easier than the emotional parts, but I didn't dwell on that. *He's here; we're both trying; the worst is behind us.*

Or so I thought ...

One afternoon, I woke up with such a terrible headache that it made me nauseous and dizzy. Tylenol wasn't touching it, so, being pregnant (with twins, no less), I went to the doctor. When we got there, the first thing he did was listen for the heartbeats. When he could only find one, he did an ultrasound.

Much to my disbelief, there was only one beating heart. Twin-to-twin transfusion is what it's called. One baby takes all the other baby's nutrients.

Laying on that table with so many thoughts running through my head made the room start spinning. I felt faint. *Is this really happening? Am I dreaming?*

The doctor patted my shoulder, hung his head low, and told me how sorry he was. *Nope, I'm not dreaming.*

The doctor left the room, and Clark and I just sat there. Neither of us moved. I was too traumatized to talk.

My ... baby ... is ... dead, I thought. *This doesn't make any sense.*

I tried to sit up to get dressed, but my body wouldn't cooperate. I scanned the room for Clark and saw him over by the door facing the wall.

"Clark?" I managed to say.

"What?" He didn't even look up.

"I need my pants."

Our hands touched as he handed them to me, but he quickly pulled back and turned away.

I sat there, almost paralyzed, as he faced the wall. I managed to get dressed and walked out of the room without looking at him. I didn't even check out; I walked straight to the car. I was worried I might lose it at any minute. I never understood what it meant for an adult to curl up in a fetal position, but it suddenly became apparent. I wanted to crawl into the floorboard of the car and disappear. *I have a dead baby inside my body—one that I was supposed to grow and protect.*

I feel like someone is stabbing my heart over and over again. My insides are shaking, and my head still hurts. I feel sick. I need to scream. I need to cry. I need to talk.

We were halfway home before I realized the car was moving. Clark hadn't spoken, or if he did, I didn't hear him. Suddenly, seeing him created an aching within me to be touched. *This isn't just your pain, Kristie. It's Clark's too. Reach out to him—and share it with him.*

When Clark used to hold my hand, I could feel the love and the peace from his body flowing into mine. When he hugged me, I would inhale and feel like I was breathing him into my soul. With my hand in his or his arms around me, I felt connected to him, and I needed that right now.

Without thinking, I reached for Clark's hand but quickly pulled back when we touched. I remembered his pulling away in the doctor's office and realized I was afraid of the rejection that followed. *Why wouldn't I be? I can't remember the last time I was vulnerable with him. I can't remember the last time he was interested.*

Clark didn't respond to the hand touch; he sat there motionless.

We drove home in silence. Clark didn't hug me, hold my hand, or tell me everything would be okay. I felt the space between us, and suddenly the gap felt so much wider. There was no denying the distance.

Why can't he look at me? Why won't he talk to me? Did I do something wrong? Say something. Anything. At that moment, I realized he was not the person I dated in high school. *He doesn't wipe my tears after sad movies; he doesn't hold my hand in the car; he doesn't hug me just because. I don't know this man sitting beside me; clearly, he doesn't even care. Otherwise, he would have tried to comfort me. He doesn't know how to help me or what I need. Comforting someone amid a loss shouldn't be rocket science.* There was so much hurt and space between us; neither of us knew how to respond. Just ignore it and don't talk about it? We were good at that.

He finally broke the silence. "Do you need anything?"

I wanted to yell, "Our baby is dead. I need you!" Instead, I said, "No." *If he has to ask me at a time like this if I need anything, that is proof that we are in trouble.*

Oh, but I did need him badly. I need human touch. I need him to hug me, hold me, and tell me it was okay and that it wasn't my fault. I need him to reassure me that we are going to be okay. I need him to step inside my pain, our pain, and feel it with me.

* * *

When we got home, I walked straight to the bathroom into my closet. I hoped he would follow me. This was the heaviest hurt I'd ever experienced, and I felt as if I might collapse.

I was aware of how badly I needed him; believe me, I wasn't too fond of the feeling, but how I felt told me I couldn't carry this alone. I'd been hurt and left before, but nothing felt as empty as losing a baby inside of me.

I heard Clark walk into the bedroom. *Finally.*

As he got closer, I turned toward him, ready to fall into his arms, but he said, "Would it be okay if I go four-wheel riding since I have the rest of the day off?"

Wait … what? What did he say? Did he ask if he could go four-wheel riding since he had the rest of the day off after being told our baby was dead? I was so taken aback by the question I didn't know how to answer. I pretended not to hear him. I swallowed hard, breathed deeply, and said, "What did you say?"

He repeated the question. The room started spinning, and I could feel my head pounding, which made it nearly impossible to think. *Tell him what you want, Kristie, and ask him for what you need. This is your chance.*

I couldn't do it; the sting of rejection felt like it might break me at that moment.

Instead, I mumbled, "I guess."

I am dying inside, and he doesn't even know it. Does he even care? Don't I matter? Shouldn't I be more important on a day like today? Shouldn't he stick around to make sure I'm okay? My baby is dead. I'm hurting, and my husband has just left me—the husband who vowed a few months ago to be the best husband ever.

It's a lie. It's all a lie. It's always been a lie. He's never going to be the man you need.

I fell to my knees on my closet floor and cried. I cried so hard and for so long that day that I couldn't cry any more after a while. My heart was broken, and my body was out of tears.

I fell asleep and woke up to the phone ringing four hours later. *My kids! I forgot to get my kids from Clark's mom.*

* * *

Clark came home that night and acted as if nothing had happened. He tried to pick up where we had left off the day before. The day before, when we were trying to repair our marriage, the day before our baby was declared dead, the day before he shattered my heart completely.

When I looked at him, I saw hurt, pain, lies, and manipulation. There is no way I could go back to "the day before." I couldn't even pretend we were going to be okay anymore. I tried, but I knew we would never be okay again the moment he walked out that door.

Lying in my closet that day forced me to recognize some brutal truths. The first truth I understood was that my marriage was dead—just like my baby. There was no coming back from this. If Clark couldn't stick around for me on a day like that, he never would. We weren't going to make it.

Clark didn't want me, and I couldn't make him want something he didn't want. No matter how hard I tried, I couldn't earn his love. It was time to accept that truth and let go.

The second truth I realized was how angry and resentful I was at Clark. I had forgiven him for so much in the past five years, but in return, all he did was mess up more—most times worse than before. I was always there for him, but all I ever got was the door. I didn't know which was worse: the fact that he kept leaving me or that I thought it was okay.

It never bothered me until that day because I kept hoping I would be good enough one day for him to stay. However, I would never be good enough for him to stay; something would always be more important than me.

Lying on that floor made me realize how mad I was at myself. *Why do I keep allowing him to do this to me?* Deep down, I knew I didn't feel worthy enough to ask him to stay. Since I felt like Clark's needs were always more important than mine, I never asked him to stay—and he didn't care enough to stay without being asked.

I felt so ridiculous. *Why didn't I realize this before? If I had, I wouldn't be here right now.* Clark had never been there for me during our marriage, so why did it shock me that he had left me again? It shouldn't have surprised me. It wasn't like this was the first time he had abandoned me while pregnant when I needed him.

The third revelation I had that day was that the hurt I had inside from Clark went all the way back to the beginning: way beyond the baby, even before the affair, probably back to college. I felt betrayed by him in so many ways, and he hadn't made any of it right or been changed by them. Why did I think I had to forgive him for things he wasn't sorry for?

I didn't, not anymore, anyway.

I also recognized that I had never recovered, processed, or healed from any of the heartbreak or heartache that Clark's affair had caused. I tried to, and I hoped to. I pretended I had, but I hadn't actually done it. All I had done was stuff it, add layers, stay busy, and pretend the bottom layers didn't exist while hoping the top layer would heal.

And do you think Clark noticed or cared? No! Just like that night, he never asked about me, how I was doing, how I felt, if I needed to talk, or if I needed a break or anything. None of that mattered as long as I kept the wheel spinning. This confirmed something I already knew: I couldn't rely on anyone, not even my husband.

Clark never asked me if I was okay the day we lost the baby, and I never told him I wasn't. I couldn't go back to the day before because I wasn't the person I was the day before.

I never grieved the loss of that baby; I refused to allow myself to think about it because it hurt so deeply. I tried to pretend it didn't happen, but death stings in a whole different way. Death's sting is a lot harder to stuff. Death steals everything from you without asking. I could no longer add layers and stay busy; my mind and body no longer worked together.

Death stings in a way that no one can accurately describe. The hurt is worse than anything any person could ever inflict upon you. Cheating, rejection, neglect, abuse, and loneliness can't touch death, and there is absolutely nothing you can do about it except pray you have someone to hold you while you absorb its impact.

But I didn't.

Everything I had ever felt was compounded that night. All my failures, fears, deficits, rejections, not being good enough, not being lovable—or even capable of doing anything right—kept hitting me in the face. I couldn't even keep my baby alive inside of me.

I did the only thing I knew how to do: take control of the things I could control and avoid or ignore the rest. I took care of myself and the girls.

I did what I had before: I shut myself down to Clark that night. It served me well the first time—or so I thought—and my instincts told me to do it again. I didn't do it on purpose or with cruel intentions. I did it to protect myself. I shut myself down to me as well.

*   *   *

In the weeks and months to come, my world got so dark that I wanted to get in bed and never come out. It reminded me of when I watched my mom do the same thing, and I had to take care of the kids. I felt sorry for her, yet I was also mad because she wouldn't get up and care for her kids. They wanted her so badly, but she wouldn't get up.

I knew I couldn't do that to my girls; they deserved me, but they deserved the very best of me. That version felt so out of reach at that time. I felt dead inside but knew I couldn't quit showing up for them. They depended on me; those babies were only two and four. I knew I had to pull it together enough to meet their basic needs. I dragged myself out of bed every morning and got them to preschool. I forced myself to eat for the baby still left inside me, and then I crawled back into bed until noon when preschool was over. After lunch, we all piled in my bed for nap time. By the grace of God, I held it together long enough during the afternoon to function for them, but as soon as they went to sleep, I curled back up in my bed and didn't come out until the following day.

I was depressed, and I knew it. Walking through each day felt like I had a hundred pounds of cement tied to my legs. Each step made my heart rate increase.

My parents came over a few times and found me in bed during the day; they said I wasn't trying hard enough because if I were, I wouldn't be having such a difficult time. Or they would say, "You've got to get over this. You are going to make the girls sad."

I always thought, *What about me? I am sad. I am hurting. Doesn't anymore care about me?* I didn't dare voice that out loud. I already knew the answer; there was no need to have it confirmed.

Clark was the only person I came into regular contact with, but he didn't seem to notice or care. He never asked if anything was wrong or if he could help, and I didn't tell him otherwise. He started working late and bought a motorcycle to occupy his time because he didn't have kids to take care of in his spare time. Whatever ... I didn't care. Emotionally, I had already checked out of our marriage. I had nothing left to offer Clark, and neither of us complained. Since he liked his time away from us more than he liked his time with us, that is what I gave him. I didn't nag him or complain. I barely spoke to him. I didn't care if he stayed. I didn't care if he left. I didn't care what Clark did. Caring took energy, and I didn't have any extra to give. The girls took every last ounce I had.

Taking care of them kept me going; they were light when everything else seemed so dark.

Clark and I were so distant by the time I went into labor that I called my friend at one o'clock in the morning, and she had to tell me to wake up Clark!

* * *

Brooke was born, and she was absolutely perfect—except that she was an absolute terror of a baby. She cried nonstop. She didn't sleep or eat. Things were already bad, and I slept to cope with them, but now I never slept. I thought I was losing my mind. No one came to help me, and Clark didn't miss one day of work when Brooke was born.

Many, many days, I thought I was losing my mind.

My dad didn't pass up an opportunity to remind me that I was the problem. He said I couldn't handle three kids. My pediatrician told me I was young, overwhelmed, and depressed and prescribed medication. I believed them; it must be me. So, I tried harder.

The thing is, no matter how hard I tried, Brooke didn't quit crying, start eating, or sleep.

Some days, I fantasized about running away and leaving everything behind, but I had too many blue eyes staring at me.

So I stayed. And I cried. I cried a lot, but I took care of my girls. I don't know who cried more: Brooke or me. I was convinced something was wrong with her, but everyone said it was just me.

Growing up, I often heard, "If it weren't for you, I wouldn't have to look at your mom," and "If it weren't for you, I wouldn't be in this situation." I didn't feel that way about my girls; I felt like they were the best thing that ever happened to me. They were certainly the best parts of me.

I didn't get upset with them, resent them, or think any of this was their fault. I loved them something fierce; instead of them aggravating me or making me feel overwhelmed, they were quite the opposite. They were my safe space. They were my peace. They were my light. I sought shelter in them. When the world felt like it was falling apart, they held it together for me.

After six months of many doctor visits, ED visits, and a few specialty visits, the hospital called late one night to let me know they found some of Brooke's urine from three months ago that indicated something could be wrong.

With the hospital's help, the following day, we had a diagnosis: renal reflux. Brooke would need surgery immediately.

The doctor told me the other girls couldn't proceed any farther down the hall.

I was dumbfounded and asked what I should do with them.

The doctor looked at me weirdly and said, "Can they stay with their dad?"

Oh yeah, I guess that's what most people do.

Clark was up for the job, though, and he did well. He was where he needed to be when he needed to be there. He would get me food and clean clothes, bring the girls to see me, and call and check on me. He didn't complain one time. He was an absolute superstar for that week. "Kristie, these girls are really cool little humans. I have missed so much, haven't I?"

Yes, and you will miss a lot more if you don't get it together. However, I didn't say that. I just nodded and smiled because they were cool little humans.

When I got home, Brooke was a different child. She slept, ate, and didn't cry much. I also slept, ate, and didn't cry as much. Life was starting to look and feel a little lighter.

Things were the same as before with Clark and me, but he now asked if I needed anything. I could tell he didn't mind helping, but I didn't want his help. I was afraid of becoming dependent on him because I was sure he was only doing it out of obligation. If so, it would wear off soon.

I was right; he quit asking. We were back in our rut. The only difference was that I had no hope of us getting out of this one. We were the calmest and most peaceful we had ever been in our marriage, but it didn't matter. I had given up on us a long time ago.

*   *   *

Slowly, those days and months trickled by and became a blur. *Thank God for that.*

Clark didn't fight for his way back in my life; he just accepted the way things were and retreated into himself. He lived his life, and we lived ours.

It was so odd not to have an emotional connection with the man you're sleeping beside, but it was peaceful. We didn't argue or fight, and I didn't nag or complain. Along the way, I realized I had no expectations for him or us and no resentment toward him. I had learned not to hope, expect, or believe things would change or get better.

Even though I hadn't healed from his heartaches or the loss of the baby, I wasn't angry with him anymore. I hadn't forgiven him either, but then again, he hadn't asked.

I learned how to block out the memories; there wasn't anything to be mad or sad about anymore. It was too much to carry back then, along with everything else, and I just let it go.

Besides, the girls were so much fun, and they kept me busy. They had reached an age that I had dreamed of. I could be an active part of their lives instead of just a physical one. Two were in school, and I volunteered as homeroom mom, with PTA, and everything else that could keep me mentally and physically engaged.

Being their mom and doing those things with them filled me. Doing that and being that made me happy and gave me my purpose.

We lived this way for two more years, but I didn't purposely avoid him or stay on one side of the house like I used to. We passed in the hallway and spoke when necessary; we even shared a giggle here and there. We went to all holiday and family events as if nothing was wrong. We were merely cohabiting for the benefit of everyone. It was easier to live this way than to do anything about it.

I thought I had found balance. If I focused on Clark, I was angry. If I focused on myself, I was sad. If I focused on the girls, I was good. I allowed the girls to fill me in all the ways I was lacking. I thought living that way was the healthiest way to go, but what did I know?

* * *

AOL and instant messenger were new, and while minding my own business, I heard the infamous words: "You got mail." Oh, how that excited me! I opened the message, very shocked by its sender.

The message was innocent enough to reply. "How are you? How are the kids?" So I responded, and eventually, one or two messages here and there turned into several messages a day, which then turned into phone calls. Since I already knew him from high school, it was easy to reconnect. We mainly talked to pass the time, but I found him so easy and refreshing to talk to. He was interested in all the things about me that Clark wasn't. How was my day? How are the kids? What's going on? Anything new?

I knew it was wrong to share the problems in my marriage with another man, but I had a longing to be loved—even if it wasn't from my husband—and that scared me. Until then, I had never thought about it coming from another source (even though I had allowed my kids to fill it in prior years).

We can overlook this longing because it's unseen or invisible—or we can tell ourselves it doesn't really exist. It's easy to get into the daily habits and routines and overlook that something underneath is driving us. That driving force is longing. Until the girls were in school, I had replaced my longing for love with their love. Until that point, I had prayed so long that Clark would fulfill this longing, and here I was, faced with a question: Do I continue to wait for Clark to hopefully one day step up, or do I take matters into my own hands?

Before I hit that send button, I felt God's Spirit inside me. I knew I needed to pray for his strength to intervene and turn myself around before I created a mess, but I had gotten far past the point of caring about consequences. Instead of praying, I just thought, *I don't think I can keep hoping for what no longer seems possible.* I justified it to myself … and I hit that send button.

* * *

You, my brothers and sisters, were called to be free. But do not use your freedom to indulge the flesh; rather, serve one another humbly in love.
—Galatians 5:13

* * *

I can see now how the unmet expectations and the longing in my heart to be loved had taken a toll on my heart. It had hardened me. I kept praying for something good, which was a reasonable request: God, fix my marriage. Wasn't that a reasonable request? I saw him doing it for others every day. Everyone else looked like they were thriving. What about us, God? Did you forget us?

We all long for something or someone. A longing, a yearning desire, is a human reality. Our longings leave us aching, and the enemy loves to use our aches to tempt us to turn away from God and ultimately turn inward to satisfy them. Turning inward tempts us to look at other things to fill us, and those are idols.

Anything that separates us from God is an idol—even good things. Anything other than God that makes the ache stop and/or makes you feel good is an idol, including food, money, success, and alcohol. Even when we substitute these things for God, they eventually leave us back on empty. Just like the gas tank in your car, when you have driven it far enough, it returns to empty, and you need to be filled again. These things will leave you restless. I know they did for me.

* * *

> Do not love the world or anything in the world. If anyone loves
> the world, love for the Father is not in them. For everything in the
> world—the lust of the flesh, the lust of the eyes, and the pride of life—
> comes not from the Father but from the world. The world and its
> desires pass away, but whoever does the will of God lives forever.
> —1 John 2:15–17

* * *

I eventually confided in this other man about my marriage. I told him everything that had happened between us. I told him my feelings about the situation, things I hadn't told anyone—not even Clark. The things I told him shocked me because I had never said them out loud, but they were the feelings I had lived with for quite some time.

"I don't think he loves me." "He just got stuck with me." "We should have never gotten married." "He's never interested in me." "He doesn't talk to me." (To name a few.)

This went on for a few months until Clark shut it down. The AOL account Clark set up for me was joint; he had been reading all the messages. One day, I came home from church, and he had a friend there waiting to get the girls and said we needed to talk. I walked inside, and he had all the emails printed on the table.

(I admired that he had found a sitter. That was a rare occurrence. He should have tried that sooner.)

As I looked at the emails, I thought, *Uh-oh, there's no going back now.*

He said, "What do you have to say for yourself?"

I just looked at him and shrugged my shoulders.

"So you're just going to sit there and not say anything?"

"You read the emails. What's left to say?"

We sat quietly for a bit, and then he said, "Why are you doing this to our marriage?"

"Our marriage?" I laughed. "Is that what you call it? A *marriage*?"

"We're married, aren't we?"

"We're roommates who happen to be married."

"If you had problems, why didn't you come to me?"

"And tell you what? What could I have possibly told you that you didn't already know?"

"You could have told me you are talking to another man while I'm working all day so you can stay home and have the life you want."

"Oh, you mean like you told me the time you were talking to another girl while I was at home taking care of the kids all day?"

"We worked through that. Why are you bringing that back up?"

"We have *never* worked through that!"

"So this is my fault?"

I sprang into defense mode. "Yes, you started this mess! Doing things a married man shouldn't be doing." And then I stopped; being right and defending myself no longer mattered. I breathed deeply and said, "Clark, I don't think it matters whose fault it is anymore. Look at our life! Look at us! Look at where we are. Does it even matter whose fault it is?"

"So what do we do?"

"I don't think there is anything we can do."

"What does that mean?"

"I think we're done."

He looked baffled. "What does that mean?"

"It means we're done. I'm done. Our marriage has been done for a long time."

We sat in silence for what seemed like thirty minutes, and then he finally said, "Do I really make you feel that way?"

"Yes."

A tear rolled down his face, and he said, "I am so sorry." And then he walked out.

*   *   *

The next day, I got up and started my typical day. I tried to figure out my plans. *Am I leaving—or is he? He said nothing about it last night, and neither did I, but that isn't shocking.*

I walked downstairs, and there he was. I was shocked. I asked, "Are you okay?"

"Yes."

"Why are you still here?"

"I figured I could help you get the kids to school this morning."

"I don't need help getting the kids to school."

"Well, I can help get them ready for school."

"I don't need help getting them ready for school either. I do this every day of my life."

"Would you like some help?"

"Aren't you missing the gym?"

"No, I didn't feel like going."

"Weird," I replied. "Because you certainly couldn't miss it when I really needed your help." *Man, that was mean, but it was true.*

* * *

When I woke up the following morning, there he was again.

"Why are you home again?"

"Just thought I could help."

"We didn't need your help yesterday; why would we need it today?"

"Well, I'm here if you need any help."

"We won't."

"Why are you being so mean to me?"

"Why do you care?"

"Because I care."

I laughed. "Our kids are three, five, and eight, and you are asking for the first time ever if you can help me get them ready for school."

"Kristie, that's not fair."

"But it's true." I giggled some more. "Clark, you are about eight years too late. Go to work."

I didn't like being mean to Clark, but being mean was the only thing that made me feel strong and in control. I am weak when it comes to Clark; no matter what my head tells me, my heart still loves him. *Why? I don't know.* But love him or not, I was tired of playing this game; after eight years, it needed to end.

When I came home from dropping off the kids, there was a note on the counter. Clark said he'd been thinking about those emails. He had no idea I felt that way and wished I had talked to him because he would have done things differently.

He told me most things I said in the emails weren't true and that he didn't feel the way I described. He told me he was sorry and asked if we could talk. He said he loved me and still wanted our marriage to work.

Talk; all I used to do was talk. Too late now, buddy. I hear you, but I don't care. There is nothing to talk about because—no matter what you say—you can't change how you made me feel. You can say you love me all day, but your words are empty if you can't hug me or hold me after our baby dies.

I didn't answer his note. I made my decision; I was done and needed to stay strong and focused. So, I ignored him and tried to figure out how to get the girls and me out of that house.

* * *

Six days later, Brooke woke up with a 104-degree fever. I took her to the doctor, and they ran a series of tests and told me to get her to the ER immediately. She had hydronephrosis—swelling of one or both kidneys—and needed surgery immediately before her kidney ruptured. I called Clark at work and told him I was scared and asked him to please come to the hospital.

Standing outside the operating room, I could hear Brooke screaming. The anesthesia should have been working. She shouldn't have been crying, but she was. I grabbed onto the railing on the wall to keep from falling and saw Clark walking down the hall. I turned away from him instantly. I didn't want him to see me crying.

I didn't want to see him, but I did want to see him. I didn't want to need him, but I did need him.

He came directly to me and hugged me.

I collapsed in his arms. I felt relieved, and I felt safe. And then I thought, *He finally learned how to hug me? How convenient.* I let that thought roll out of my mind. I needed that hug—we both did.

He held my hand while we sat and waited for the doctor to come out. He even wrapped his other arm around my shoulder. He kept telling me that Brooke was going to be okay. I felt less alone in his presence. It was such an odd feeling from Clark, but it was comforting. *When was the last time someone hugged me or told me it would be alright? I can't even remember, but I'm happy he's here.*

Brooke stayed in the hospital for a week, and when I got home, I couldn't think about my plans to get a job and my own place. Those plans would have to be put on hold. I had a sick child who needed me home.

Did all of that happen to prevent me from leaving? Things happened at the worst times, and I couldn't make sense of them. Maybe I was being punished by God for what I had done.

I had no idea about anything anymore. All I was sure of was that I needed to take care of my kids, protect them, and love them. I was okay with that because I knew how to do that well. Loving them was easy. I would stay and endure whatever I needed to for their sake.

When I got home, there was another note from Clark. He reiterated everything he said in the last note except with more detail. He said he should have been a man and fought harder for our marriage. He begged me to stay and try again, and he promised to get it right this time. He talked about us being a "real couple."

Maybe he is serious. He promised me communication, date nights, and everything he had read in my emails that he knew I longed for.

This time, the letter hit me differently. Maybe Clark wasn't the only one to blame anymore. I was guilty too. *Shouldn't I forgive him if he is willing to forgive me? Maybe this is a perfect opportunity for a new start. Perhaps we aren't done just yet. If Clark has changed on the outside with his lifestyle, he may change on the inside too. If he can change, I can too.*

* * *

Five years have passed since that Christmas Eve that forced me to see the devastation and destruction within my marriage and to acknowledge the heartache, the lost hope, and the unmet expectations. And it has been two years since I owned up to being responsible for contributing to the mess. Clark and I have changed so much individually and in our marriage, but at the same time, not at all.

We have been trying so hard, emotionally and physically, this time. I never knew loving someone took so much work; it felt like a full-time job. *I don't think either of us knows how to do this correctly.* Everything felt like trial and error. We worked so hard, but something always happened that threw us back to square one. *It's so draining.*

We were trying hard to forge forward. I'd learned to ignore the past and not give it any headspace. Clark seemed like he was okay too. In those days, his life looked a lot like mine. We went to work, came home, and cared for the girls. We went to church on Sundays. What more could I ask for?

Well, I thought nothing, most times, but sometimes life felt a little too programmed. It felt like we were doing what we were doing out of obligation rather than because of love or because we enjoyed it. He was always with us but still not with us (if that makes sense). He wasn't very interactional with any of us. He seemed to think his presence was enough.

Roll call? Here. Check.

I wanted all of that, but I wanted *Clark* to want all of it and not act like he was in jail while doing it. And that's what I felt like.

Sure, he had given up everything I had asked him to, but he also seemed miserable because of it.

We now had three older kids who looked to us for answers and guidance. They demanded our time and attention in a whole new way. They asked questions when things didn't feel right, and they expected explanations.

They were observant and would call us out. "Daddy, why weren't you at my game?" "Mommy, why are you crying?" "Daddy, why aren't you going with us?" "Why are y'all arguing?" There was no pretending around them anymore.

They held us accountable; they challenged us to be different and to do better because we both wanted to be good parents.

It was scary though; we saw those fragile lives in our hands and knew we were responsible for them. Talk about intimidating!

I think Clark felt like the young and immature stages of his life had ended and were no longer acceptable because I saw the changes in how he thought, behaved, and responded. He was trying. Bless his heart—he was trying.

I was also trying. My priority was on those girls, but I was also working on my marriage. I was like Chicken Little though, I automatically assumed the worst whenever something happened and prepared for it. If we argued, we were getting a divorce. If Clark was late coming home, he was at a bar. If he didn't answer his phone, he was with another girl. That kept my emotions all over the place. My guard was always up, and my defense mode was always on high alert.

I knew this about myself and wanted to change it. I practiced slowing down and assessing the situation before I jumped to conclusions. I tried talking less and listening more to avoid assuming so quickly.

Clark and I worked hard not to feed off each other's emotions; we both understood that one of us had to remain calm and rational so things didn't escalate like they used to.

However, no matter how hard we tried to change, do better, and be better for our marriage and our girls, we couldn't get the marriage part. We weren't arguing or fighting, but we weren't talking either.

We didn't have honest, authentic communication or talk about our hopes, dreams, or future. We needed to be growing and evolving together, but we weren't.

Unfortunately, I was still waiting on those date nights he promised.

One day, Clark overheard me telling the girls that we needed a bigger house because of their toys. That night, he said, "Would a bigger house make you happy?"

I don't know if it will make me happy, but it will make life more comfortable. I guess comfortable could equate to happiness.

I had never thought about a bigger house, but without much thinking, I said, "It would."

He said, "Well, let's make that happen."

Subconsciously, I think Clark and I both knew we needed something to look forward to; otherwise, we weren't going to make it. We needed a change, some excitement, something to distract us. *We worked well off of distractions.*

We started the search for a new house the next day. The thrill of the hunt was fun. It was exciting, it took us out of the monotony of life, and it spiced things up a bit.

We started communicating—genuine, non-forced communication—and dreaming about the future. We talked about what we wanted in the new house and what purpose it would serve. We finally had something to look forward to! (My word, I can still remember the excitement).

We both felt like we were healing from the past and carving a new future, and we liked it. It felt so good to have the gloom cloud removed from over our heads. I started to feel connected to Clark for the first time as an adult.

We eventually found the perfect house; it was big enough for our family to grow up in and bring all their friends. It would be great to host in—we didn't have any friends, but we had big dreams—and it was beautiful.

It really was a dream house because I had never dreamed I'd live in something like it. The only downfall was it was older and needed remodeling, but Clark could do all of that and enjoyed it. We bought ourselves a new house.

The house was so big that I told Clark it would take us ten years to finish it, but I didn't care. It was exactly what we needed: something to connect us.

Or so I thought.

* * *

We poured ourselves—and every spare minute and dime—into that house for the next two years. Clark gave up his motorcycle and all other hobbies, but he really just swapped them for working on the house. All he did in the evenings and on the weekends was work on the house. He didn't go anywhere without us anymore, but he didn't go many places with us either.

I was getting frustrated with how things were going, but what upset me the most was the girls' longing for their dad and his absence.

When I fussed at him, he would remind me that he had bought this house for me. Soon the peacefulness had left, and things started getting tense between us again.

One of the things Clark has always done that drove me mad and made me feel terrible was if he came home and the house was messy, he would plunge into cleanup mode before saying hey. He would give me the silent treatment until "operation cleanup" was complete and at least an hour had passed. It was like I was being punished. And the moods, oh my, the moods that accompanied it.

It was all so disheartening.

In the earlier years, when he wasn't around as much, it didn't happen as often because, well, he wasn't around. Now that he was home, it made him bonkers, which drove me mad—and made me feel like a failure as a wife. We constantly argued about the house, and it was not messy!

He would get mad and shut down, which hurt my feelings. I would get upset and shut down. Eventually, we arrived back at exactly the place where we started in our marriage: avoidance, hurt feelings, lack of communication, and arguments.

The house had become our biggest source of contention. I kept telling myself that we were still learning and growing, or I could have admitted there was a real problem. The real problem was that the house was just another way for us to avoid the real problem. The real problem was the hurt, the pain, the distance, and the disconnect. The house was just a Band-Aid, a cover-up to distract us from dealing with the real problems and possibly even healing.

But I wasn't ready to admit we had a real problem, not just yet, anyway.

CHAPTER 5

STOP THE RIDE

On our tenth anniversary, I got my parents to babysit for twenty-four hours. I had dinner reservations and imagined it would be a celebratory event. Ten years is a long time! I envisioned what a wonderful time we would have, a kid-free dinner at that. It had been a long time since we had done that. We would talk, reminisce, and dream about the next ten years together. We would laugh and giggle and exchange gifts. It would be a fantastic night—the end of one era and the start of another. I was excited at just the thought of it.

Kristie, I don't know whose marriage you envision, but it's not yours.

It can be. We have been doing well lately.

Hmm …

Okay, the first ten years hadn't been magical or even close to good. Maybe okay at best.

Clark says I have expectations for how things should happen, and I get upset when they don't play out as imagined. He's always telling me I can't get mad if things don't go as planned. Maybe he was right, but even if I had low expectations for our anniversary night, they would have been better than what actually took place.

To start with, he spent the whole day cleaning and organizing his garage. That was supposed to be *our* time. I was frustrated but said nothing since I didn't want to ruin the night. Instead, I went to the mall to get something new to wear to dinner. I wanted to look super nice to impress him. I'm not sure he even noticed me most of the time.

I got dressed and felt good about myself. I hoped he would like what he saw, but as soon as I walked out the door and down the steps, my heel got stuck in the step—and down I went. I imagine it looked something like the scene from *Miss Congeniality*, except I didn't bounce right back up. And I don't look like Sandra Bullock.

Well, he didn't notice me that night either. All the hard work and effort I had put into my appearance that night was for nothing. There was not a single comment or compliment on my new outfit or that I had put on makeup and fixed my hair, which was a rare occurrence. My feelings were hurt, but I was determined it would be a good night.

We drove in silence, but I attributed most of that to trying to decide if my foot was broken. The pain was unreal, but broken or not, this night was happening.

Unfortunately, things didn't get any better during dinner.

I kept asking questions to get a conversation going, and he answered them, but he didn't initiate any other conversation outside of that. I resorted to telling him stories about the girls even though I wanted to talk about something different for once. I assumed that would engage him, and he would jump in and start chatting, but that didn't happen either.

I was staring at the walls in silence and trying not to make eye contact with him because I was holding back tears. Watching other happy couples giggling and chatting away around us struck me. *Our marriage is in trouble again.*

I could feel the sting of that thought, and I felt my face begin to burn. *Don't cry, Kristie. Don't cry. That would be embarrassing.*

By the time dinner was over and we got to the car, I was frustrated, and the sadness I had felt inside the restaurant was gone. I regained control of my emotions and asked, "Is everything okay?"

Shocked by the question, as if he hadn't just sat through the same dinner I had, he said, "Yes, why?"

"It doesn't seem like you are happy to be here or with me."

"I am," he replied with no questions or concerns about why I was asking those questions.

"Did you have fun?"

"Yes."

My head about snapped off my neck as I turned to look at him. *That wasn't fun; that was awful. Who even is this guy? And what rock is he living under?*

"Clark, you never talk to me, and that bothers me. I can't remember the last time you initiated a conversation or came and sat beside me to be near me." *How do I get to know a man that won't talk to me? How do I live with someone I don't know?*

You've done it for the last ten years.

Ugh.

He just shook his head. No response.

"Are you even happy? Do I make you happy?"

A little angry or bothered, he mumbled, "Here we go again."

"What does that mean?"

"Why do you always accuse me of not being happy? If you aren't the one happy, then tell me, but quit accusing me of being unhappy."

"It's just that you don't seem interested in me in any way. And you never want to know anything about me." I could feel a lump forming in my throat. *Don't cry. Stay strong.*

No response. He continued staring straight ahead at the road. That was the end of the conversation. I wasn't sure if he was thinking about what I said, if he didn't want to argue, if he didn't have a reply, or if he didn't care. I don't know because he didn't respond.

We drove home the same way we went there: in silence. This time, it wasn't my foot hurting; it was my heart.

Once again, I was left to form my own conclusion, and my conclusion hurt my feelings. It told me the worst. I felt like I'd been trying to fill the gap between us, but he wasn't meeting me in the middle. *We get along fine until I bring up things I would like to change in our marriage—like communication, feelings, or time spent with me—and then he shuts down, just like tonight. Where do I go from here? Things just aren't getting better.*

Maybe you should quit asking for things you know he can't or doesn't want to deliver.

But I don't want to live like this for the rest of my life.

We got home and went to bed in complete silence—*a not-so-happy anniversary.*

I was starting to get angry; it would be on when I used to get angry. I used to yell, scream, and pick a fight until he finally gave in and started talking to me, but I stopped that long ago. I didn't like that version of me anymore, but I'd be lying if I said I didn't think about picking a fight to get him talking. I was dying to know what was going on inside his head, and I knew that was probably the only way I would get those feelings out of him. But I didn't.

I couldn't do it. I didn't want to do it. Instead, I did the only thing I knew to do when I got upset. I withdrew. But still nothing. Complete silence. I knew where it was going: exactly where it had gone so many times before.

I don't want tonight to go there. I don't ever want to go there again. I'm so tired of us living this way.

So don't.

Don't? What does that mean?

Leave.

Leave? I can't leave. Wait … can I leave?

Do you want to live like this for the next ten years?

And that thought ended our tenth-anniversary celebration.

* * *

Last week, I had to go to my parents again to intercede. Twenty-three years together, and those two haven't changed one bit. I wonder if Patty knew then what she knows now if she would have stayed.

Will I be wondering the same things about myself one day? What if I spend another ten years hoping and praying for my marriage to get better, but it doesn't? Then what? I've wasted twenty years of my life. Should I waste another ten years of my life waiting? Hoping?

If we are this disconnected now, what will we be like after the kids are gone? I don't ever want to be like my parents. We might not physically fight, but I don't want to end up in a loveless marriage.

It's already loveless.

That thought knocks the breath out of me.

We love each other. It's not loveless.

Then what is it?

I don't know, but we're not like my parents. We're not repeating the same bad choices over and over and putting our kids in the middle of it.

Then what are you doing?

Hey, our marriage has gotten better over the years—not worse!

Has it?

Yes, we don't argue or fight anymore.

But you don't talk either.

We are trying!

Are you?

At least we're making it work for the kids.

Have you ever thought that your kids will grow up someday and have their own opinions and ideas about marriage—and what you've shown them will highly influence that?

My sweet, precious girls, I want nothing but the best for them. I would never want them in a situation like mine or my parents'.

What will your kids say about your marriage when they get older?

I don't know. My situation isn't that bad.

Then why are you complaining?

I want my husband to act as if he loves me. I mean, I want my husband to love me.

He says he's doing everything you ask him to do. When will you ever be happy?

I want him to be happy too. I want to be more than roommates. I want a teammate.

Ugh, Kristie. You are always wanting more. Look at where you are. You have gone from teenage parents to a six-figure income in ten years. You've overcome many obstacles and made your way up the social ladder. Can't you be content with what you have and be thankful for the changes both of you have made?

Yes, but…..

But what?

Is asking for my husband to love me too much? The only dream I've ever had was to get married and have a family, but I did not envision it looking like this. I am thankful for the life I have. It's the marriage I don't love.

I know you want a Hallmark movie, but those aren't real!

I am happy. I am content. I love Clark, but I am not in love with him. And Clark is not in love with me. I can sit and argue this all day long and defend my stance or even justify it from any angle, but the truth is that this is not the life I envisioned for myself. Clark and I are both good people who are trying to do the right thing, but how much longer do we keep trying for the sake of the girls? I know we wouldn't still be together if it weren't for them. Would they thank us for staying in a marriage for their benefit— or would they rather I leave and be happy, like I wished for Patty for so many years?

Why are you even still here?

Because I'm scared.

Scared of what?

Leaving. What if I leave, and it's the worst decision ever, and I mess up all of our lives?

What if you stay, and it's the worst decision ever? What do you want, Kristie?

I want a husband who loves me, values me, and invests in our family and me.

Do you have that?

No.

Can you attain that one day?

I don't know, but I keep hoping and praying.

What do you have right now, Kristie?

A marriage of contentment.

Is that enough?

Sometimes.

Would it be enough to wake up at forty with only a marriage of contentment? The children will be long gone.

No.

Do you think Patty thinks her marriage of contentment is enough now? Do you believe her staying shaped her entire being and those around her?

Yes. Oh, my! I've got to do better for my girls. I want to be an example for my girls to follow, but if they see me the same way I see Patty, then nothing changes. I can't just tell them. I have to show them. I need to be the example I want my girls to model: fearless, independent, strong, worthy, and loved.

How do you become those things?

I don't know, but I have to find out because I fear they will repeat the same generational mistakes if I don't.

Maybe if someone had been brave enough to show your mom, stepmom, or aunts, one of them might have had a different life—and their children wouldn't be repeating the same things you are right now.

Yes! I see the toxic generational cycle. I feel the pressure on my soul. This has to stop. Someone has to be the cycle breaker.

* * *

I made a list of pros and cons. The only pro of staying was God and the girls, and I was beginning to believe that the girls would be okay if we split.

The more I thought about staying, the heavier it felt. I feared waking up almost forty, wondering where my life had gone, and I asked which was worse: living with the regret of something I did or didn't do?

I started feeling like time was running out and that a decision needed to be made soon. Since I didn't want to make this decision alone or blindside Clark, I tried to talk to him about my feelings. I talked to him the only way I know how to: state the facts, tell him how *we* feel, point out the obvious, and don't be vulnerable.

I said, "Clark, I don't think we are happy. We don't communicate as married people should, and we aren't emotionally connected. We don't have fun together, and we never laugh or spend time alone."

He said, "I don't have a problem with our marriage, but if you have a problem with it, then maybe you should talk to someone about it or do whatever you need to do. Just stop blaming me and accusing me of having a problem with our marriage."

"You don't think we have issues in our marriage?"

"You are the one who has the issue. I don't. And you have some deep-rooted issues that are all you, not me."

Well, that didn't go very well. Deep-rooted issues? What in the world? That's a new one. What does that even mean? Deep-rooted issues?

Believing him, I started seeing a therapist.

* * *

My therapist asked me what I wanted out of a marriage, and I said I wanted a helpmate. I wanted a friend. I wanted someone to talk with, dream with, yell on the sidelines with, joke and laugh with, and someone whose arms I could melt into whenever I had a hard day. Someone who excited me to tell them about my day, someone who actually cared about it—or me. Someone to be silly with, someone to go on adventures with, someone to help me raise and guide our kids.

"How many qualities of those does Clark possess?"

"None."

My therapist looked at me as if I were exaggerating and then asked more questions. After I answered them, she looked at me seriously and said, "What has kept you in this marriage this long?"

"Mainly the girls and my belief in God," I said.

"Is your marriage a God-honoring one?"

Staying in my marriage is honoring God. "God doesn't like divorce."

"God doesn't only tell you to stay married; he tells you to honor him through your marriage."

Well, I'll be.

"What would you tell one of your girls if they told you what you just told me about your marriage?"

"If their marriage made them feel about themselves like mine does, I would tell them to leave."

"But would that be honoring God?"

"Ha ha ha. I see what you are doing. They're different though."

"What makes them any different from you?"

"They deserve to be loved."

"Don't you deserve to be loved?"

"I want to be loved."

"But do you deserve to be loved?"

"I … don't know."

"What don't you know?"

"I don't know if I've earned it yet."

"Have your girls earned it?"

I had never considered whether my girls had earned the right to be loved. I just knew they deserved to be loved because they existed—and my love for them automatically made them worthy. I tried to explain this to her the best way I knew how.

"So you think love has to be earned?"

"For me, yes, it has always had to be earned."

"Why?"

"No one has ever loved me just because I existed. No one has ever valued me or made me feel worthy without working for it."

"So you must earn love from someone to be worthy?"

"Yes."

"What happens if they take it away?"

"You try harder."

"Are you afraid to be loved?"

"No."

"Do you think you can earn Clark's love?"

"I keep trying."

"Look, I can't say if Clark loves you, but love isn't earned. Love is free. Love is a feeling. It's not based on what you do or don't do. Just like with your kids. But if Clark doesn't make you feel loved, and you know that you have been trying to break the barriers between y'all, and he isn't responding after ten years, then chances are he isn't going to."

That was not what I expected to hear today. Not. At. All. "So, what do you suggest?"

"It doesn't sound like y'all have much of a marriage, but if you aren't ready to see that, I suggest couple's counseling."

"I thought you were going to help me fix the problem. Clark said I was the problem."

She looked directly into my eyes and said, "Honey, you can't fix a one-sided marriage. Get him in here for couple's counseling."

I think I've been hit upside the head. Is this what therapy is like? I assumed she would ask more questions about my marriage since that's why I came. I had answers about that. I could have told her everything Clark did wrong, but I didn't know the answers to the questions she kept asking about me. *Those are hard. I don't want to talk about me. I don't like therapy.*

*   *   *

I told Clark what the therapist said, and he said, "Are you seriously still mad about our anniversary night?"

"It's not just about that night, Clark. It's about our entire marriage. This is exactly why we need counseling. You don't listen when I tell you how I feel."

"I thought you were talking to her about you. I didn't know you were talking to her about our marriage."

"Seriously, Clark?"

"Kristie, I don't have a problem with our marriage. We don't need couple's counseling."

"Clark, you don't think our marriage needs help?" I could tell he was getting frustrated.

"I gave up everything for you. I stopped doing everything you complained about. I do everything you ask. I buy you whatever you want. But none of that is good enough. Those are your issues, not mine."

"Are you kidding me, Clark? Did you say you gave up everything for me? All you gave up were the clubs, the alcohol, and the girls. Should I bow at your feet and praise you for giving up something you shouldn't have been doing in the first place?"

"Whatever … you're impossible to talk to."

"Is that why you don't talk to me? Well, since you buy me everything I ask for, maybe I should have asked for communication for our anniversary—and then we wouldn't be having this conversation right now."

"Oh, we would still be having this conversation because we have it every other day."

"Maybe when you said giving up everything for me, you were talking about when you got me pregnant and had to marry me."

After a long pause, he said, "Kristie, that's not true."

"Well, it took you long enough to answer. Maybe I'm not the only one with some deep-rooted issues."

*   *   *

The Lord himself goes before you and will be with you; he will never leave you nor forsake you. Do not be afraid; do not be discouraged.
—Deuteronomy 31:8

*   *   *

The realization of what Clark said and the therapist's words, "You can't fix a one-sided marriage," led me to make a follow-up appointment.

"Clark will not be joining us today or ever," I said as I walked in and sat down.

"So what are you going to do?"

"I don't know. Isn't that why I'm paying you?"

She giggled.

I like her. She's direct. She's sassy and confident. She knows exactly what she wants and how to get it. I admire that.

"Tell me more about you and Clark. What were things like before marriage? How did you meet? What was dating like?"

I started from the beginning and told her everything from dating to our current state.

She scrunched her face, raised one eyebrow, and said, "I think you and Clark have what is considered a 'push-pull' relationship."

"A what?"

"A push-pull relationship. It's when one partner seeks greater connection but grows critical when the connection is elusive. The other partner seeks greater autonomy but withdraws in the face of complaints and pressure."

"I have no idea what that is."

"In relationships like this, one partner doesn't have a sense of love for themselves, and they're challenged to become involved in a structured, secure relationship, often pushing the other person away after pulling them in."

"Ugh, that explains why I would pick fights with Clark for no reason when we were dating. I always wanted to understand that. Clark once asked if I was deliberately trying to start a fight, and I thought that was the silliest thing he'd ever said. Why would I deliberately start a fight?"

"Well, keep in mind that for a push-pull relationship to keep spinning, both partners are active and responsible for contributing. If one partner stops contributing, the relationship dies."

"I'm so confused."

"You are both responsible for this. Both of you lack self-confidence or have lower self-esteem than most. One of you has abandonment issues, and the other has a problem with intimacy—and these fears create these push-pull mechanics."

"I hear what you're saying, but I don't understand."

"Kristie, we aren't trying to fix a one-sided marriage anymore. This isn't a case of 'I love him, but he doesn't love me,' which is what you originally presented."

"What is it then?"

"You both have some codependency issues that run much deeper and will require you to work on and fix—or the marriage isn't repairable. Push-pull relationships are toxic. The people involved in this type of relationship typically have unhealed wounds from previous experiences or have been exposed to unhealthy relationships, causing them to develop unhealthy attitudes about relationships."

She hit the nail on the head right there! My family is absolutely toxic, and I guess Clark and I are pretty unhealthy too. "So, what can I do to fix this?"

"Kristie, you cannot fix this marriage on your own. However, you can own your part and fix yourself, but as I said, when one person stops contributing to a push-pull relationship, it dies. If you don't get Clark in here, your marriage has no chance of survival."

"He said he wasn't coming to therapy. I told you that."

"Well, then you need to learn what a push-pull relationship is so that you can understand what is happening or has happened, and then you will be able to see how it has evolved to where you are now."

"How long is this going to take?"

"As long as it takes. You can't rush this. There are no shortcuts. Growth and healing take time."

"I don't know how much time I've got."

She rolled her eyes. "By its simplest explanation, the pusher will be the one to initiate the relationship, and the puller will avoid it for fear of being vulnerable to abandonment. This sets the entire tone for the varied stages that make up the cycle you have endured throughout your relationship."

"Are you sure we have this? I don't think Clark has ever pushed or pulled in this relationship?"

"Kristie, you have a classic case of this. All the cycling and its stages confirm it."

"What do you mean by cycling and stages?"

She handed me a piece of paper. "I will go over this with you. I want you first to listen, don't interrupt, make any thoughts, or think about how you want to respond. Just listen. Then we will dissect it in parts, and you can ask questions and take notes. It may take us several sessions, and that's okay. I want you to hear what I'm saying, really hear it, before we can begin to work on it. Don't worry about getting Clark to come with you. Leave that alone for now."

Over the next month, I met with my therapist, and she explained what a push-pull relationship was, and she was correct. Clark and I totally had a push-pull relationship.

*   *   *

Turns out Clark and I have been in this toxic cycle of this "push-pull" relationship for more than ten years. Who knew? Even dating, I can now see how we have taken turns being the pusher and the puller. I remember once when, I was about to leave, and Clark showered me with gifts and attention. I wallowed in the gushing, creating that false sense of security. After that happened, the roles reversed; I had the upper hand because he thought I would leave.

My mind flows with so many of these situations. I see now, I hear it, but I cannot understand it. Why? Why did we participate in this for so long? Why would we choose to live this way? Why didn't one of us stop it? My therapist says we're the perfect storm, but I don't think there is anything perfect about us.

*   *   *

I asked my therapist, "If this is so toxic, why does it continue?"

"Cycles continue because a need is being met. Wounded individuals seek other people or things to satisfy their unmet needs. It's not fulfilling, healthy, or stable, but it's better than what they see as the alternative: being alone or feeling the pain."

"Why do Clark and I both continue in this cycle?"

"Because it's working. This cycle has developed a routine for you to maintain a marriage without meaning or substance, and it doesn't sound like either of you wants anything deep or intimate. Neither of you wishes for the marriage to progress too seriously, nor do either of you want it to end. You want it to be sustainable—your way."

"That's not true," I say. "I want intimacy and deep connection with Clark badly."

"Then stop the cycle."

"How do I do that?"

"Stop the ride and get off."

Stop the ride and get off? That sounds silly. Wait ... does stopping the ride mean getting a divorce? "I don't want a divorce."

"That's why I said you want sustainability."

"Well, I don't anymore!" Suddenly, it made sense to me, and I agreed with what she was saying. I could see how sustainability had been all I was seeking—shoot, maybe that's all my mind could comprehend—but I didn't want it anymore. I truly wanted everything from the marriage I told her about in the first meeting. Maybe I wasn't capable of that during my teens and early twenties, but I felt I was now. I wanted it. "Am I allowed to ask Clark for more than sustainability now?"

"Kristie, you're allowed to ask for whatever you need."

"I am?"

"Sometimes, in toxic cycles, the emotional upheaval becomes too much for a person, and they decide to leave it behind. And sometimes, a person grows and changes, and this cycle no longer works for them. It only takes one person brave enough to make a change to stop the cycle." Either she saw the wheels spinning in my head, or smoke was coming out my ears because she said, "Kristie, get Clark in here for couple's counseling."

* * *

Once again, Clark saw no need for couple's counseling. He was convinced I was the only one with issues that needed fixing. He said, "Do all the therapy in the world that you need to do. You fix you, and I'll fix me."

I can't fix a one-sided marriage. Hmm ... there is no way I can fix myself and think this marriage will work.

What are you going to do, Kristie?

Well, I know sustainability is no longer working for me, my life, or my marriage. I want more, but I'm afraid this marriage is stunting my growth. If I have the power to stop this madness, then I need to do it. I think I would rather regret the decisions I made than the ones I didn't make. I do not want to spend the rest of my life wondering. If there's a chance I can rise above where I am now—mentally, physically, and spiritually—then that's a chance I want to take.

Are you sure about this?

Yes! I owe it to my girls, especially. And who knows, Clark might even thank me for this someday. We might even find love and happiness again.

I walked into therapy and announced, "I'm going to stop the ride."

"Finally," she said. "Now we can work on your backbone."

I giggled as if I knew what she meant.

* * *

Our rental house became available, and I thought, *This is my sign. I need to leave now. Otherwise, I never will.* It felt like the right thing to do, but it also felt so wrong. I had gotten over the stigma of a divorce—something I swore I never wanted to do to my kids—but I had difficulty accepting that I was letting God down.

That was the part that felt wrong and heavy. For years, I had begged God to heal my marriage and fix us, and he hadn't.

"Maybe that wasn't his plan," the therapist said.

I believed her, but I knew divorce wasn't his plan either. I couldn't understand his plan for my marriage, which was frustrating. Maybe she was right. Perhaps it was time to fix myself, heal, and make myself happy. It didn't seem like anyone else would help me in that area.

I wrote a note, packed a bag, and left.

Dear Clark,

This isn't exactly how I imagined our goodbye. In my head, it was way more dramatic. Probably one of us would have gotten caught cheating again, or we would have fought about something you did wrong and how I nagged you to the point of fighting back. So that you know, I always liked when you fought back because that was the only time I ever knew your true feelings. Those were your moments of truth. I wish there could have been more of them. Not the fights, but moments of truth. Without those moments of truth, I was left only to create scenarios in my head of your truths. I'm sure I created whatever truth worked to my advantage. And then I would react to that. I am sorry for that. In my defense, you didn't leave me much to work with. Communication was never your strong suit. Being vulnerable was never mine. I guess we're all a little broken.

Anyway, when you read this, I will be gone. And I am sorry I could not tell you this in person, I have never been able to look you in the eyes and leave. Believe me, I have tried several times. I am sorry, I really am, but, Clark, I cannot live like this for another ten years. We just celebrated (if you call it that) our tenth anniversary, and it was pitiful. It was sad. It seemed so forced. And it's not just one-sided; it seems mutual that neither of us is happy. I know it seems as if we have lived this way much of our marriage, if not all, and what's so silly is we have finally learned how to cohabitate peacefully together. So why am I doing this now? I don't really know, Clark, except the thought of living this way for the next ten years scares me to death. It scares me more than writing this letter. I can't do it, Clark. I can't live this way for another ten years, and I don't want to. I have to believe there is more to love than this.

Marriage is supposed to have love in it, but we just cohabitate.

Marriage is designed for intimacy, but we barely talk.

Marriage is supposed to be teamwork, but we do our own things and go our own ways.

Marriage is designed to be holy and to glorify God, but ours insults him.

Marriage is intended to be a refuge from the outside world, but the storm is inside our marriage, so we seek the outside world for refuge.

I feel that we have completely wrecked each other, wasted the past ten years of our lives, and have nothing to show for it except bitter memories. I know that sounds harsh and dramatic, but it's how I feel when I think about us. I know we tried extremely hard to repair the damage in the past two years, but the problem is that it is unrepairable. Too much damage has been done. I know we love each other—we have since we were fourteen—but we aren't in love with each other. We could live like this, housemates for the sake of the kids, pretending to be happy, and maybe one day we will. Who knows? I know we have found contentment and peace, which is much better than the arguing, the fighting, the silent treatments, the worry, and the wondering, but it's not enough anymore when I think about the rest of my life. It's just not enough, and it's so much work for no payout. I guess what I'm saying is, I am done. I'm exhausted. When I admitted all that to myself, I somehow found hope again and feel that if we end this now while we're still young, both of us will find true love and real contentment. No matter how much I try to pretend or tell myself I don't need someone to love me, I want someone to love me. I want someone to do life with.

Anyway, when you read this, I will be gone. I'm staying at the rental house. I will give you a few days to process this, and then we can sit down and make a schedule for the kids. We also need to decide how to proceed forward with a legal separation.

Please don't call me tonight.

I truly am sorry,
Kristie

I folded the note with his name on the outside and left it on the dresser. I took one last look around the room as if I was telling it goodbye. Maybe I was—or perhaps I was hoping for something to convince me this was the worst decision I'd ever thought of. I knew in my heart it wasn't though. I knew it was time to go. Our marriage had gotten much better than in the beginning, but it was still pathetic. I didn't care who I was letting down—not even God. Indeed, he would understand. I forced the thought out of my head, turned, and walked out.

I walked down the steps, out the door, and to my car. As I pulled out of the driveway, I thought, *There's no turning back now.*

I did not make this choice lightly. It was one of the most difficult choices I'd ever made, and I doubted and second-guessed myself for months. Decisions have always been hard for me because I'm always wondering what others will think, how it will affect them, and how it will make them feel.

In making this decision, I did not talk with anyone about it. And I did not tell anyone when I did it. No one except me, Clark, the girls, and my therapist knew for the first month. I felt too ashamed to tell anyone—like a failure—but I knew I had made the right decision.

As soon as I walked through the front door of my own house that night, I felt like the weight of the world had been lifted off my shoulders. I started crying. For the first time in my life, I felt free. I slept that night without worrying, wondering, anxiety, or fear. I had no expectations of myself or anyone else. I was done with trying and failing.

Ironically, no one knew, yet it was the first time I felt like I wasn't living a lie.

CHAPTER 6

LIVING SEPARATE LIVES

I thought leaving was the hardest thing I'd ever done, but staying away proved to be much harder. Clark said he respected my decision to leave, but he used the same line I had used years ago: "Just because you don't want to be a part of this family anymore doesn't mean the girls should have to leave their home." (And I thought he never listened?)

I assumed Clark understood that if I left, the girls would also leave. I didn't think he would fight me over custody, but much to my surprise, he said his house should remain the girls' permanent home for the time being since I didn't have solid plans yet. *I have solid plans!*

Clark said the girls needed stability and to see us both equally. I agreed. He said we needed to think of them and not ourselves, and I also agreed.

Clark suggested we do the one-week on and one-week off rotation. This idea didn't allow the girls to stay in his house full-time or give them the stability he insisted that only his house could provide them.

Clark then suggested the three-day, four-day method, which left us with the same dilemma and took me away from my kids for days. Clark knew my resistance on this issue, and I wasn't budging. I would not go days without seeing my kids or allow my kids to see me. I would rather come home and be miserable than do that.

I thought long and hard about going home and how it would be the easiest and best option for the girls. *If you give up now, Kristie, you will return to the same situation you just left. Besides, Clark didn't ask you to come home.*

Finally, after countless hours of conversation and many weeks of trial and error, Clark and I adopted a plan that we felt was best for the girls. We decided we would work around them instead of them having to bounce back and forth between us. Clark and I would pack our bags and swap houses every other weekend instead of the girls. This gave them stability, kept them in the same routine and house, and gave us equal time with them.

Clark would do the mornings with them and take them to school, and I would pick them up and resume our regular day-to-day routine. When Clark got home, I would leave and go to my house. I fed them and did homework, and Clark did bath time and bedtime.

It sounded easier than it was. I had never been away from my girls, and Clark had never kept them alone. That part frightened me, but I knew they were safe—and it was crucial for Clark to bond with them during this time. My therapist pointed out that I had taken valuable time and opportunities away from Clark and the girls by doing it all in the past. They should have been bonding and growing with him the whole time.

The transition was rough. I said many "I don't knows" to the girls when they asked me questions, and I didn't like that. I wanted to be able to promise them it would be okay, but there were times I wasn't sure I believed it myself because I didn't know how to be a grown-up. I didn't know how to be a single mom. I didn't know how to be independent or alone, and I didn't know how to share my kids.

I didn't have any friends or family to help guide me or even be supportive. At the end of each day, I was all I had. I had to be my own cheerleader and keep reminding myself that it wouldn't always be this hard. I was learning as I went, but things were always conflicting, which made everything questionable.

Learn what needs to get done, and it will get easier. This is just a season.

I quickly learned that things were more complicated on my own than I expected.

There is the reality of your car breaking down on the interstate while you are out of town, and you have no idea what you should do. It is a big inconvenience to deal with the silly things that your husband used to take care of, but you are a big girl. Now that it's your responsibility to figure it out, you do.

And that's what I did—I figured it out. Day after day, I kept going. I learned so much. I was determined to become self-sufficient. I transferred everything into my name, opened my own checking account, and began paying my own bills.

I learned how to operate a lawn mower and dealt with everything that broke. I even bought a new car, all by myself. I was so impressed with myself.

But no matter how many things I learned or taught myself, there was one thing I could not master: quietness.

Of course, I knew the nights would be quiet without the girls, but I was not prepared for what it brought along with it—loneliness.

The quietness made me think, and thinking made me feel, and I didn't want to think or feel. I tried focusing on the future instead of thinking about the past, but that was so difficult. I began to see that staying busy helped me avoid this situation, so I immediately tried to find ways to fill my time.

Even that became a challenge since I didn't have a life, friends, or hobbies. I would work on the homework my therapist gave me for the week, but that was all I had to do to pass the time. There was no mess to clean up and hardly any dishes or laundry. I didn't have cable, and social media wasn't a thing. Cutting grass became my new hobby.

Of all the things I anticipated being difficult, quietness was not one of them.

One night, I looked over and saw my Bible. I reached for it and started reading. I had to stop my mind.

Reading my Bible that night created a lot of curiosity. I suddenly had questions I had never thought of and wanted answers to. I went to the bookstore and bought a new Bible with commentary. The commentary helped me start to understand things differently and more clearly. I was so intrigued with what I was learning that I started reading my Bible every night.

Clark never did ask me to come home, and I'm so glad he didn't. I don't know if I would've been strong enough to say no, especially in the beginning. It was just so lonely, but the loneliness forced me to stand in the hard spots.

The loneliness tried to take me down, and I almost let it. I thought it was my worst enemy, but it would turn out that loneliness was precisely what I needed to get where I was going.

* * *

About a month into this, as we were swapping out the kids, Clark asked if this was what I really wanted. I was shocked because, up until that point, he hadn't questioned me about my decision to leave.

"I think it's for the best, but, no, this isn't what I wanted."

He nodded as if he understood but said nothing.

That question bugged me all night. I wish Clark could have elaborated on it or told me what he was thinking. I didn't want him begging me to come back, but I didn't feel any lost love, which hurt because the decision had hurt me badly. *I wish he knew how hard this is for me, but would it even matter?*

Deep down, I still loved Clark and wondered every day if we could've salvaged our marriage somehow. I didn't make the decision to leave because I had someone waiting for me or offering me a better life. I made the decision in the hope that each of us could somehow salvage ourselves for the benefit of our girls. We couldn't attain that together, and I thought it was for the best, but it still hurt deeply. I didn't sense that it was as hard for Clark as it was for me, which gave me more determination to continue.

The girls became my focus and the strength I drew from. I wanted to be a mom they were proud of. I wanted to be better for them and offer them more. Staying in that marriage in a constant state of distress took so much attention away from them because I was constantly trying to figure out how to fix it. I thought, *If I fix it, it will fix us as a family.* I wanted to be able to lead and guide them spiritually and wisely. I wanted to be the mom for them that I wished I had. Keeping that in the forefront of my mind was my perseverance.

I talked to my therapist about these feelings, the confusion, and the loneliness, and she suggested journaling. "Journaling will allow you to put your thoughts into words and recognize the feelings you're running from. You need to think, journal, and process. It's part of therapy."

The following week, I told her, "I don't like that journaling junk—even if it is part of therapy."

"Why not?"

"All these feelings and memories keep coming into my head and make me feel worse."

"Journaling requires you to sit with yourself, to be honest and real. That brings out hidden feelings and can help you heal."

"I don't see the point of it, and I don't like how it makes me feel. I'm not doing it."

She giggled. "You can't outrun your mind forever, Kristie. Eventually, it will catch up to you."

I need to run faster, I thought.

*   *   *

Clark had to work late, and he called and asked if I minded staying late with the girls.

"Of course not," I said.

He then asked if I minded if he went out for a drink with the guys afterward.

I swallowed hard, and memories flooded my brain. *Clark, bars, friends, drinks?* I felt a tear fall. *He's really moving on.* I felt sad and hurt. My therapist pointed out that I am hardwired to go into defense mode to protect my feelings, and we've been working on this, but instead of applying what I had been learning, I went straight into defense mode. "Clark, you can do what you want. You're a grown man. You don't have to ask for my permission. You never have anyway. Why start now?"

I shouldn't have added that last part, but the thought of him moving on hurt. *But isn't that what he's supposed to be doing? You don't want him back, so what's the problem?*

"Okay then. If I'm too late, sleep in the bed, and I'll crash on the couch."

"Whatever. Have fun," I said sarcastically.

I got the kids to bed and went out onto the back porch. It was so pretty out there; it overlooked the water. I thought about the house and how it had been my dream. I had so many visions for the house when we bought it, and now I wasn't even living there.

I don't think the house itself bothered me; it was the lost hope that the house represented. The house showed me that love couldn't be bought, imagined, or pretended. It showed me that love was so much more and that we both deserved it. Looking at the house was just a reminder of our failed marriage.

As I was deep in thought, Clark walked in the door.

"Nine o'clock?" I said. "What are you doing at home at nine? And you're still standing? That's impressive."

"Ha ha, funny one. It wasn't as fun as I remembered, and I wanted to be home with the girls like I should be."

"I am here. They are fine."

"I know, but this is where I want to be."

Interesting. "Well, if you ever want me to take them to my house so you can go out, I don't mind. That way, you won't feel like you need to be here."

"Thanks. I appreciate that."

Clark has always been a man of few words. He doesn't ask you to explain things you say or defend himself. I'm not sure if this is a good quality or if he doesn't care enough to engage in my passive-aggressive comments.

"Hey, you can still have the bed tonight," he said. "I'll take the couch."

"Nah, I should go home."

"You sure?"

"Yes, I'm a big girl. I'm sure."

"Drive safe."

Why did part of me want to stay? Why did he ask? Did he want me to stay—or was he being considerate?

Quit thinking, Kristie. Quit thinking. It doesn't matter.

Since Clark went out after work, I wondered if this would be recurring. I had told him I would watch the kids, and he did have my permission even though he didn't need it. Maybe it was time for me to go out? *Is that okay? Am I allowed to do that?*

I laughed at the thought. I didn't even know how to go out. I had never been on an actual date. What does going out even mean? I giggled at the thought of me drinking at a bar. *Kristie, you don't even like the taste of alcohol.* I was deep in thought when a vision of Clark at the bar with another girl popped up. The idea of Clark out with guys didn't bother me, but that thought made me sick. How had I not thought about that possibility? *Not again, Kristie. You knew this would happen. You even said you hoped both of you could find true love.*

I wanted him to be happy, but the thought of him with another girl is too much to think about.

But it's reality, and you must imagine it to get used to it. Isn't that what people getting a divorce do? Find other people? They don't usually live the rest of their lives single.

Yeah, but so soon? If that's the case, we need to file separation papers to make it right. We need to be legally separated, on the way to divorce, before I can imagine him with another girl.

I thought about talking to Clark, but what would I say? "Hey, I know we're separated, but I wanted to know if you thought we should get legally separated?" How weird would that sound? Of course, we needed to separate legally. I found a name in the phone book and scheduled an appointment.

*   *   *

I arrived at his office, scared to death. When the attorney asked me questions, I immediately felt my face on fire. I was on the verge of tears, but I was fighting them hard. *Be a big girl, Kristie. Be a big girl. You've got to be a big girl.* It was way more emotional than I imagined it would be.

He explained the fees and how you must be legally separated for a year in South Carolina before filing divorce papers.

I knew most of it from hearing others' stories.

He looked at me and said, "Are you sure you want to do this?"

As I nodded, I burst out crying. I could not understand what was going on inside of me. All the emotions! *Things are going so well. If Clark and I can be as good as we are now but divorced, that's great.*

He said, "Are you sure about this?"

Nervously, I giggled and said, "Yes."

He said, "Most people sitting in your seat aren't crying when they fill out divorce papers."

I gave him another fake giggle.

He said, "I'm going to ask you one more time if you are sure this is what you want to do because if this is what your husband wants, then I would make him file, and he would have to pay for it."

I shook my head again and said, "It's okay. I want to do this."

He looked confused. "Do you mind if I ask why you are crying?"

"I don't know. It just seems so real … and that feels so sad to me."

"Divorce papers are real. They are final and expensive, but the good thing about South Carolina is you have a year to change your mind."

As sad as it was and as heavy as it felt when he said that, I thought, *A year is so long to draw this out.* "Can we not make this happen quicker?"

"Not unless one of you is having an affair … and you must prove that."

I shook my head.

He gave me another serious look. "Little girl, I don't think you know what you want—so a year is probably what you need. We will draw up separation papers, you sign them, and we will have him served unless you think he will sign them for you. Once he signs them and you return them, we will file with the courts, and your year separation will start. Once the year is up, we will set a court date for the final divorce hearing."

The main thing I heard was "little girl." I was trying to get it together and not appear *so little.* This was all new to me. I had never been in an attorney's office alone. It felt very daunting. I looked at him and said, "Okay, let's get this started."

I left that office not feeling anything like I thought I would. Doing that did not make me feel any better about the situation. Those papers I carried felt heavy, and the reality felt heavier. Once those papers were signed and filed, our lives would be cut from each other forever.

All of a sudden, I couldn't imagine life without Clark. But, then again, I couldn't imagine life with Clark anymore. *This is normal, Kristie. Every divorced couple has once felt this way.*

I had so many thoughts storming through my head that I couldn't tell the difference between the ones I believed and the ones I was trying to make myself believe.

How can I be sure I'm making the right decision when it hurts this badly?

It hurts because you don't know anything other than Clark. You have been with him since high school and never dated anyone besides him. These are normal feelings. Things will continue to move forward, and you'll find a new normal.

One thing I did know for sure was that I didn't miss our marriage. After being out of it, I didn't think I could ever go back to it. Life was not meant to be lived that way. Other than the few hiccups I've encountered, I liked the life I was creating for myself and the girls.

I learned that day that part of "figuring it out" meant learning how to think things through and make a decision. I had to trust my choices and not look back, regardless of whether they turned out to be right or wrong. That was irrelevant; what was relevant was that I made the decision based on the best information I had.

I had to learn to trust myself. The only way to trust my decisions was by refusing to second-guess myself and playing the what-if game.

Look at you, Kristie! You did a big thing today—all on your own. Trust yourself. Trust the process. You're doing great!

Yes, I can actually do this adulting thing alone.

It was all so unnerving at first. Every first big thing felt excruciating, overwhelming, and painful until I tackled it, and then it didn't feel so bad. I came to realize that fear comes from standing in the unknown. All I had to do was move.

Once I took the step and felt what it had to deliver, it didn't feel so bad—even if it was painful.

* * *

I casually left a copy of the separation papers beside his bed that day with a note: "Sign these when you get a chance and give them back to me."

He called me that night, and I was sure it was to talk about the papers. Maybe he didn't like the agreement. I gave him absolutely everything except custody of the kids. I didn't ask for half of the house, his 401(k), alimony, or any of our assets. It said he could have it all, which my attorney advised against, but I didn't want to fight. We had done that our entire marriage. I wanted our future to be as smooth as possible for the girls, and if that meant giving him everything, I was willing. I only asked for primary custody of the kids, but it said we could do fifty-fifty.

I swallowed hard, bracing myself for this conversation.

Instead, he said, "I want to talk to you about Katelyn. I talked to her tonight, and she is struggling more than she lets on. Maybe you can take her somewhere alone this weekend. I'll keep the others so y'all can talk."

We discussed this in more detail and thought of some ideas to help her. We talked in great length about being more aware of the girls' needs—even if they seemed to be doing okay.

It was a strange conversation to have with Clark. It was maybe the first time I'd discussed the girls' needs with him. I had always handled that independently, but having someone with a vested interest to run thoughts and ideas by felt good.

I had always felt parenting was my solo job because they were girls, and he was never around, and when I did tell him something, he usually just said, "Hmm."

I told him I appreciated him taking the time to call me and talk about it and how nice that felt. We hung up without even mentioning the separation papers.

* * *

While I was at Clark's house after school with the girls, he called and said he wanted to tell me something. I figured it must be serious if he needed to tell me from work. I walked outside to get away from the girls.

He said, "I want to be respectful since we are getting along so well. I would like that to continue, so I'm trying to ensure I don't do anything that would ruin it."

"Okay," I said. "I appreciate that. What's up?"

"I am going to ask someone out to dinner, and I wanted to tell you before I did it."

I sat down. My legs suddenly felt light, and I thought I might fall. The sky started spinning. *Wow, he didn't waste any time. I guess he was ready to move on. That's why he's been so nice. He's already over me.* I reminded myself that I was over him too—as if that would make me feel better—but was I ready to date other people? *He's prepared for his next chapter of life to start.*

"Kristie, you there?"

"Um, yes, I'm here."

"Is that okay?"

"I appreciate you telling me this, but you don't need my permission, Clark. That's why I filed the separation papers … so we could restart our lives. And you don't need to tell me from now on. I don't want to know if you go to dinner or what you do with other people … just don't do it around the girls."

There was silence as if we were both processing this.

Finally, I said, "We are good, Clark. We are doing a good job co-parenting, and the fact that you wanted to tell me this makes me feel like we are heading in the right direction. But there comes a point where we don't need to know everything the other is doing, and this is that point. That's why I filed those papers. You are free to do as you please … and so am I."

I said that stuff to appear strong, but I'm not sure I believed what I was saying—even though it was true. Clark was free, and we were getting a divorce. A spark of pain ran through my chest as I swallowed those words.

"You are right, Kristie, but I want to be respectful—and I wanted you to hear about it from me first. You can do as you see fit, but I will continue to do what is right and be respectful of you because you will always be the mother of my children."

"I know, Clark, and as much as I appreciate it, I just don't want to know. I can't imagine you with another girl. It hurts too much." *I can't believe I said that. It's true though. It does hurt.*

"It hurts? Why does it hurt? This was your idea."

"I know, but it still hurts. I love you, Clark. I have always loved you. It was our marriage I didn't love." *I can't believe I just said that either.*

"Well, I thought we were trying, but you were the one who just got up and left without any warning."

"Wait, what? Did you want to stay in that miserable marriage for the rest of your life—or would you rather be where we are now? You certainly seem happier now, and you sure aren't having any problem moving on."

His voice got louder. "This is not what I wanted, but if this is where we are, I might as well start to figure it out."

My voice got even louder. "And you are off to a great start, Clark."

"Kristie, you are the one who left. If you don't like this, then come home."

Wait … what did he say? Come home? Does he want me to come home? Don't go there, Kristie. Don't go there. You are only going to get hurt. Stick with the plan. You are doing so well. With my voice much lower, I said, "Clark, we both know you don't want me to come home."

"Kristie, I just wanted to tell you myself. I thought it was the right thing to do. I'm sorry if it upset you. I don't want to argue or place blame whenever we need to talk about something important."

"You are right, Clark. It was the right thing to do. I am sorry for how I responded. I am confused about how this is supposed to work. This is not how I wanted us to end, but I suppose I can also show respect and tell you when I get to that point."

"Thank you, Kristie."

I replayed our conversation over and over in my head for days. I heard mixed signals, but he retracted them quickly. *But did he?*

Was he trying to tell me something? And would it matter if he was?

We could never fix this mess before—and we've only made it worse now. Let it go. But what did he mean by come back home?

Let it go, Kristie. Keep moving forward. Think of the work and how exhausting it would be to try. Besides, Clark just told you he would start dating. Why would you think he wanted to get back together?

The conclusion to my conversation with myself told me Clark had confirmed he had no problem getting over me—and he wasn't heartbroken about the impending divorce.

I had battled internally for years over this situation, beaten myself up over walking out of our marriage and whether it was the right thing to do or not, wondering if I would scar the children or hurt Clark. But knowing there was no love lost punched me in the gut.

I had hoped he might try harder to save our marriage for our family, but why would he do that now when he wasn't interested in doing it before?

Even though I thought I had it all figured out, I still saw my therapist once a week. And thank God because she was the only person I had to talk to. I'm pretty sure she kept me sane, but when I told her about our conversation, she pointed out a few *little* things about me.

She told me I was needy, insecure, couldn't make decisions, relied on others for validation, looked for love and acceptance in others, was a perfectionist out of fear, felt rejected and abandoned, and was a people pleaser.

"Wow! Are you sure you don't have any more you want to add to that list?" I asked.

I was devastated to hear her say those things, but deep down, I knew she was right. *I don't like hurting people because I don't want them to feel bad. I don't like being mean to people because I want them to like me and accept me. I want everyone to be happy—and I will make myself unhappy or uncomfortable to make them happy. I make myself available to others at my own expense. I tell people what they want to hear so they won't leave me. I do what people tell me to keep the peace between us. I don't like people being mad at me because that means I have failed them. It all comes down to this: I need to be liked, accepted, loved, and wanted.*

It was sad and pitiful. I was relieved that I had not realized any of that until then because learning that in an unhealthy state would have completely broken me. Learning it without the help of someone to help me understand and process it would have left me even more lost and confused. I finally felt ready to learn the truth and accept it. I was ready to apply it to my life, change, and become the person I wanted to be for my girls.

*   *   *

I went on several dates. It was so bizarre to be twenty-eight and not know how to act or what to expect on a date. What do you talk about? I quickly realized I hated small talk. I don't care about the weather or the news. I want to know about you. Are you my type? What do we have in common? I felt like dating was a waste of my time. I knew I wasn't ready, but I also knew I would probably never be ready.

Dating intimidated me. I was fearful for many reasons, which wouldn't allow me to ease up. I felt so serious. Someone said, "Just go and have fun." *What does that even mean?* None of the dates were fun. They were stiff and awkward. I hated stiff and awkward—even though I knew I was the awkward one.

Other than the dating nonsense, I was happy. I had advanced at work, which included a raise, and that helped me tremendously. Having a job and being able to provide for myself and the girls made me feel good in a way that I'd never felt. Confidence is crucial—whether it's an illusion or not.

Clark seemed happy. The girls were doing well. Clark and I got along so well that we started doing the kids' activities together, which was weird because he had rarely joined me before. He and I talked about life, how we felt, and what was happening. We were respectful and honest about what was going on in each other's lives. It was amazing, truly amazing, how this was all playing out.

I knew I was changing. I felt better about myself. I enjoyed the girls on such a deeper level. I could talk to them with a freeing mind, and I didn't feel stressed. I felt like I was a better mom without all the distractions.

Clark was changing too. I hadn't thought about this happening, and it surprised me. He lost weight, bought a new wardrobe, and bought a new car! And he seemed happy. I didn't care about the clothes, the weight, or the car, but the happy part, I must admit, cut me to the core.

But why? I wanted him to be happy. I was happy and had moved on, creating another life without him. I was glad that he was doing the same. Why did seeing him happy bother me? I don't know. I would have felt worse if he had sat around and cried all day, so his being happy was a good thing.

I think it was the reality that I couldn't make him happy. That was my life goal for so long, but I couldn't make it happen. Seeing him happy reminded me that I was still a failure. If he had found someone else, and she made him happy, which brought about the change in him, then that meant I wasn't worth changing for.

Wow! That realization stung hard, but the bottom line was that we couldn't make each other happy. We had tried for ten years. We had three kids together. I wanted him to be happy so he could be the best version of himself for the girls. *That's all I should be concerned about. He's happy. I'm happy. This is the way it should be.*

No matter how much I changed in other areas, when I saw Clark, I remembered how I had failed us. I felt like I was back in high school again, trying to rid myself of my longings and codependency on him. I needed to close that chapter once and for all, and I was determined to make it happen this time.

About a month later, a drug rep I knew from work asked me out. I had known him for a while; he was handsome, nice, and had a great personality. Charming. He was fifteen years older than me, which seemed weird, but we talked so easily that it didn't bother me. *Hmm, maybe this could be fun and not as rigid or awkward as all the other dates.*

Immediately, I knew I liked him. We just hit it off. I never understood that phrase until that night. We talked for hours the first night. He was so easy to talk to and funny. He *really* talked to me, and he asked me about me. It had been a long time since someone was interested in me or my life. He asked me about the girls. He had his life together, and he was financially secure. I didn't necessarily have a list of what I was looking for, but he seemed to have all the right things if I were to have a list.

The feeling must have been mutual because he asked me out again and then again and again until he was the only person I was going out with. It wasn't awkward with him at all. He fascinated me. He seemed so confident. It was not in an arrogant way; it was in an "I'm comfortable with myself" way. Maybe that's what happens when you get middle-aged; you find security in yourself. I'm not sure, but I liked it.

Regularly turned into exclusively for the next six months. I really fell for him. He was everything Clark was not. We talked and started dreaming, envisioning how to merge our lives. He made me feel special, heard, valued, appreciated, and loved. He made me feel important. Other than when Clark and I were dating in high school, that was the first time I felt important or that I, as a person, mattered.

I introduced him to the girls. That was very weird. It felt wrong but good at the same time. I thought, *My girls shouldn't have to do this.* They handled it like champs. They liked him instantly. I mean, he was hard not to like.

Things were going so well that I thought something would go wrong at any minute. *This guy isn't going to be who he says he is. He probably has a secret family that I don't know about.* I had lived my entire life waiting for the bomb to drop and everything to explode, and I was constantly on guard, but that never happened. I was the happiest I had ever been. I felt like a real person. I felt alive. I wondered, *Why didn't I do this years ago?*

* * *

Today I am twenty-eight and alone. This is the first time I haven't spent my birthday with Clark in fourteen years. It's bittersweet, but I see life evolving for both of us—in different directions. And I guess I have to be okay with that.

I'm trying to decide if I feel like celebrating. I'm conflicted between feeling like there's no reason to celebrate alone and feeling like I want to celebrate myself, even if I am alone. I'm so proud of how much change I have endured in the last six months. I feel like a new person, and I am proud of that.

I know this is hugely related to the new therapy I have been doing, but it is hard work, and I'm the one who's been showing up, and because of that, I suppose today should be celebrated, even if I do it alone.

Cognitive behavioral therapy (CBT) has changed my life. It gave me the tools to change how I think, act, and respond. It has taught me how to identify my faulty ways of thinking and reevaluate them in light of reality. It has helped me understand the patterns of my unhealthy behaviors and the motives behind them.

My mind feels more transparent and unrestrained. It has significantly slowed down. I can process my thoughts before they come out of my mouth and send me into a frenzy. I have more control over my emotions and can move from immediately reacting to slowly responding.

Learning new coping and processing skills has changed my perspective. There is no more pretending things are okay or wondering and worrying if today will be good. Today is exactly what I decide today is going to be. Taking my thoughts captive and deciding how to respond to them instead of allowing them free rein has been life-altering.

Little by little, some of the lies I believed about myself are dissipating. *I am capable. I don't need control. I am enough all on my own. I can make my own decisions.*

I also second-guessed myself every single day. When you are transitioning out of an unhealthy state, you can feel good and doubt yourself at the same time. I am moving forward, but I've only taken a few steps. I'm proud of those few steps, and I am going to acknowledge and celebrate them. But I won't stop here, I'll keep doing the work as long as I need to. This is for me. Happy birthday to me.

Cheers to change!

＊　＊　＊

My therapist kept telling me how proud she was of me. She always told me how strong and brave I was becoming, pointing out how I was breaking generational cycles and becoming a new version of myself. A better one. A stronger one. She made me feel like a rock star. Ten feet tall and bulletproof. She had me believing I was in control of everything in my life.

"If it's meant to be, it's up to me," is what she kept telling me.

And I kept believing her.

It felt so good to be making someone proud. I had no idea she had become my idol—or that I had replaced Clark with her. The more she doted on me, the harder I worked to change. I was still seeking validation, acceptance, and approval from someone. I just didn't know it, but God did.

I was in the process of learning that I needed to face my fears instead of avoiding and denying them, so my therapist suggested that I visit my mom in West Virginia. It had been almost eight years since I'd seen her, and she had just gotten out of jail.

My therapist thought this would be a perfect opportunity to practice this new life skill. *Nothing like a little exposure therapy.*

I expected my mom would be a little more excited to see my kids and me, but she wasn't. She hardly got out of bed or acknowledged my presence. The reality hit me like an arrow straight to the heart: nothing had changed since childhood. She would never want me or love me like I needed or desired, and I needed to accept that.

I left her house that day and vowed never to go back again. I would not set myself up for that kind of hurt again. *Every single time, she lets me down. Last time, I said it would be the last time, but no. Why do I keep doing this to myself? Why did I think she was ever going to change? Why would she love or want me now if she didn't love or want me then? Whatever, I'm twenty-eight years old. I don't need a mother anyway. I made it this far without her. I'll make it the rest.*

As soon as I got through the mountains and had cell service, I called Clark. I needed to feel wanted and loved. I'm not sure why he was the person I chose to call, but he made me feel worse.

"I'm sorry your visit was awful. That stinks. Well, be safe coming home."

I was mad at him. I had hoped talking to him would make me feel better, but it didn't. I thought, *How come every time I need someone in my life to lean on, no one is ever there?* I felt myself going down the rabbit hole and knew I needed to use my new coping skills, but I decided to pray instead.

God, why can't you give me someone? Anyone. Just someone who cares about my feelings, wants, hopes, dreams, and desires. You gave me a mom who didn't love me. A dad who didn't want me. A stepmom who didn't like me. A husband who was burdened by me. Will you ever provide me with someone who will accept, want, or love me? Will someone ever choose me?

While praying, I heard a voice: "I want you. I chose you; I died for you."

I dismissed the bigness of that voice because I did not understand it. It would be some time before I would learn how to believe that—really believe that—and let it change my life.

* * *

The following day, the psychiatrist I worked with asked about my visit. He knew the history and was curious. As I retold the story, I could feel my eyes tearing up, and I fought to hold them back.

"Being a motherless daughter is hard. Don't pretend it isn't."

"I'm not! I'm doing the work. I faced that fear, it didn't kill me. I'll be okay."

"Have you talked to God about it?"

I shifted in my seat.

"I'll take that as a no."

I rolled my eyes.

"You're struggling with your faith, aren't you?"

"No, I don't think I'm struggling with my faith. I'm struggling with my sin."

"Are you talking to your therapist about this?"

"No, we don't talk about faith or religion."

"But your faith has always been important to you."

The dam of tears I had been holding back burst. "Well, look where that got me. Besides, the more I read my Bible, the more I believe it was the law I had been most concerned with—not faith. I don't even know if I had faith."

He looked me straight in the eyes so profoundly that I felt it penetrate my soul. He said, "You are in a spiritual battle right now, and you need a Christian therapist, one whose beliefs are better aligned with yours. You need to have someone speak the truth and point you back to your faith. You may have wandered, but you do have faith. You can't see it because you've been listening to someone who has you believing in your own strength, abilities, and self-help. You need to be free of your people-pleasing ways—but not replace it with self-reliance."

He got up and left the room.

Okay then. That was weird; it was as if he were reading into my soul—or he's a psychiatrist or something.

I ran to the restroom to hide until my face returned to normal color. In there, I prayed, *Dear Lord, return to me my faith or give me renewed faith.*

When I returned to my office, I found a piece of paper with a date and time, a woman's name, and a message: "She's expecting you tomorrow."

So, I got a new Christian counselor.

CHAPTER 7

BEGINNING TO RECOGNIZE THERE WAS MORE

It only took a few weeks for my new therapist to identify something that would change my life completely. This information would help me understand things I had never considered before. This statement pierced every piece of fiber within me and stung so severely that my body felt as if it were on fire: "You need to deal with the trauma of your childhood."

When the words came out of her mouth, I suddenly couldn't breathe.

"I believe your traumatic childhood has leaked onto your teenage decisions and bled onto your marriage, and I believe they are still greatly hurting you."

I felt like all the air in the room had been sucked out. "Trauma?"

"Trauma shapes us whether we intend for it to or not."

"Doesn't everyone have a colorful childhood?"

"Trauma is tricky because it hides in the dark and jumps out at us when we least expect it. It tries to convince us that what we experienced was normal."

"But … childhood trauma?"

"By its simplest definition, trauma is a deeply disturbing experience or series of experiences. If you have been abused—mentally, physically, spiritually, or sexually—been neglected, lost a loved one, or survived an assault or a natural disaster, you have experienced trauma."

"I know my childhood was dysfunctional, but I never considered it traumatic."

"Kristie, you can't neglect what has shaped and formed you. Clark isn't the only person who has hurt you, but he's the only one you've been able to blame."

"What does that even mean?"

"You have some deep-rooted Kristie issues you are fighting; it isn't all Clark.

"Kristie issues? Why does everyone keep saying that?"

"You know why. We've touched on them before. You will have to pull them to the surface and deal with them. Otherwise, you will blame Clark for the rest of your life so that you can remain the victim."

I was confused. *Victim? I am a victim.* I didn't dare say that.

"Kristie, you had a pretty traumatic childhood. Nothing you have told me is normal or okay. You experienced abandonment, neglect, manipulation, mental anguish, and physical and mental abuse. You were the scapegoat of your family. You watched your dad physically and mentally abuse your stepmom your entire life. This list goes on and on."

"But ... trauma?"

"I know you have been working on yourself with your former therapist and processing your impending divorce, but we can't neglect what has shaped and formed you."

I let out a nervous laugh and shifted in my chair.

"What's so funny?"

"Every time I come to a new therapist, they tell me something unrelated to what I'm coming for. My first therapist was supposed to help me process *my* issues, but instead, she convinced me my marriage was the problem, and now I come to you for spiritual guidance, and you tell me I had a traumatic childhood."

"Maybe this is where God needs you to be to start truly healing."

"God needed my marriage to end so I could learn how to process my childhood? That sounds silly to me."

"Maybe God isn't done with your marriage."

"Oh, I'm pretty sure God, Clark, and I are all done with that marriage!"

"Hmm," she said.

She is right. I would never label it trauma, but my childhood still greatly affected me. I didn't trust because of my dad, and I refused to be weak or vulnerable because of my mom. Watching Patty showed me what mistakes not to make. I knew these things, so why did I need to process them? Why can't I continue reinventing a new me and bypass that other junk? That's what my first therapist was helping me do.

"But I don't talk to my parents anymore—so why must I process this?"

"Kristie, to become the healthiest version of yourself, you must process the past and heal from it fully. You can't just avoid it for the rest of your life."

"Why not?"

"Because it will always have power over you if you don't."

"It doesn't have power over me," I said loud and sarcastically with an eye roll.

"Are you sure? You don't trust, you don't love, you don't ask for help, you don't have friends, you think you're in control, you avoid anything or anyone that makes you feel vulnerable, and you're pretty good at walking away when things don't serve you anymore. You don't seek closure, forgiveness, restoration, or reconciliation; instead, you leave so you don't have to face hard or uncomfortable things. And you're teaching your daughters the same thing."

"That's not true," I exclaimed.

"How is it not true?"

"I left toxic situations. My dad hit me when I was eight months pregnant; we would have fought to our death if Clark hadn't pulled me off him. What was I supposed to do after that? Ask him how he felt about it?

"My mom abandoned me. She never wanted me! Was I supposed to keep going back, hoping she might change her mind one day? Well, guess what? I did, and it turns out she hasn't. So what do you suggest I do about that? Let me guess? Pray about it—or maybe I should offer her some forgiveness."

She had struck a nerve. I was crying at that point.

"What about Clark?"

"What about Clark?" I said so defensively that I felt like I was hollering. "I tried for ten years in that marriage, and I forgave him many times. I tried reconciliation and restoration or whatever you call it, and he didn't want any part of it."

"So you stayed with him until you no longer needed him."

"That's a low blow," I said. *I'm done. This conversation is over.* I stood up to leave. *Uh-oh. She is right. I am a runner.* I turned around, but I refused to make eye contact with her. I stood silently for what seemed like forever. I looked at the clock, and we still had twenty minutes. *Ugh!*

Change, Kristie. Change. You promised yourself change this year. She is here to help—let her.

Watch what you say, Kristie. It will be used against you.

Change, Kristie. Change. How badly do you want it?

I looked her directly in the eyes and broke the silence. "I loved Clark—I still do—but the problem is that he never loved me."

"Do you think he would have stayed for ten years if he didn't love you?"

I never thought about that question.

"Kristie, you have so much pain and hurt inside you. I don't think you can separate what's true and what's a lie. It has so much power over you."

She's not telling me anything I don't know. But what I don't know is what to do about it.

Suddenly, I felt so broken—maybe more so than before I walked through her door. *You need help, Kristie, more than you can offer yourself. That "If it's meant to be, it's up to me" bologne isn't working anymore. Let go, Kristie, and let God.*

I felt a peace come over me that I'd never experienced before. I breathed deeply and then exhaled. I knew it was my time to jump. It was time to leave my comfort zone and trust God.

I took a seat. "I do not want anyone or anything having power over me. Someone or something has controlled me my entire life. I can't take it anymore. That's one reason I left my marriage."

"Good. Are you ready to break these strongholds and walk out of bondage?"

"Yes," I said quietly.

"It's going to take hard work."

"Work? I'm used to working. Sign me up if it will bring me healing." I looked up and gave her a little smile through my tears.

She gave me a sweet smirk. "Continuing to stay broken is easy; anyone can do it. You will remain a victim and bleed onto anyone you come in contact with. Healing is hard, but it stops the pain and the bleeding."

My eyes met hers, and I held the gaze. "Am I bleeding onto my girls?"

She didn't say a word, but she didn't have to. The answer was written on her face.

I had no clue I was dripping onto others, especially my girls. I suddenly felt sick. *I have to change. This has to stop.*

"I need to stop bleeding. I can't stain my girls."

"Healing will not be just about you, Kristie. It will be about your entire life."

*   *   *

A nurse friend told me that for extreme burn victims, they bandage all their wounds, and after an hour, they go in and pull them all off and do it again. Again and again and again. She said there isn't enough morphine out there to stop the pain they feel when she has to rip off that bandage. It bothered her so badly that she almost quit her job; the pain she saw in those patients was too much for her to handle. Their screams haunted her.

One day, she finally asked, "Why is it necessary to keep ripping off those bandages all day long? Isn't once a day enough?"

"No," the doctor said. "That's how they heal. Every time you rip off a piece of dead skin, they are one step closer to healing."

"How? When you pull off all the skin, aren't you just exposing the wound once again to the same state it was before?"

"No, when you pull off that dead skin, you get rid of the damaged skin. You have to continue pulling off all the dead skin in order for them to heal correctly. If you leave the dead skin on while they are still healing, the body will heal over the dead skin, which can create infection and all sorts of problems later. Sure, they would heal quicker if we didn't keep pulling off all the damaged layers, but they wouldn't heal effectively—and long-term health is the goal."

That story describes how I felt during therapy with my new counselor. Every week, I showed up, and I felt like she was pulling off so many wounds that I might die from the infection. At times, the pain was unbearable. I had no idea I felt some of the feelings I spoke about. I felt so exposed and vulnerable. I was ashamed and embarrassed. Surely, I reeked from the smell.

*   *   *

I will give you a new heart and put a new spirit in you; I will remove
from you your heart of stone and give you a heart of flesh.
—Ezekiel 36:26

*   *   *

Things I Learned during This Separation

To start the healing, I had to identify the scars and bumps. Once I did that, I took away half of its power. Then I had to begin understanding how it had affected me and what I've carried and believed as a result of it.

During the next few months, my therapist identified many areas of my life that needed to be processed, worked on, fixed, or put to death.

Healing is a journey because the next steps involved understanding who I was, who I wanted to be, where I was, where I wanted to be, and what changes it would take to get me there. Quickly I learned that I might have the correct information, but I couldn't get the transformation desired if I didn't apply the knowledge to my daily life.

Applying the knowledge required work. That season was the most brutal I'd ever experienced, and I felt like quitting every single day—but I'm so glad I didn't because it taught me so much about life, myself, and God.

*   *   *

First, I learned that I needed to deal with the trauma of my childhood.

I had to acknowledge that I was psychologically and physically abused during childhood, and I had to quit pretending it didn't happen and minimizing the situation. I had to accept that I wasn't responsible for it then, but it was now my responsibility to reclaim control and peace over my life.

I learned to accept that I had been neglected and abandoned as a child, but that didn't mean I wasn't loved or wanted. There is a difference. I had to figure out what accepting it truly meant.

Acceptance meant I got to decide what to do with it. I had the choice to let it rule my life or let it go. Since I had lived long enough being a victim, I knew it was time to let it go.

Letting go didn't mean the feelings would magically disappear. No, plenty of hurt and emotional toil still existed, and I would have to work through that, process it, and put it to rest.

Letting go meant I no longer allowed my painful memories and experiences of a lousy childhood to rob me of living a good life now. Just because I accepted it didn't mean I embraced my trauma or agreed with it.

I learned my feelings of helplessness carried over into my adulthood and made me feel and act like a perpetual victim, causing me to make choices based on my past pain.

My therapist said, "When you're a victim, the past controls your present. But when you've conquered your pain, the present is controlled by you." She went on to explain. "There may always be a battle between your past and present, but you must be willing to let go of the old defenses and crutches you used as a child to navigate your trauma."

I had to learn new coping mechanisms to change.

Our childhood primarily affects our beliefs, which dictate how we treat those around us or allow others to treat us. Our past experiences have made us who we are today, whether we admit it or not, but the good news is that we don't have to remain those people.

* * *

I learned who I am in Christ.

I'll never forget the first session with my new therapist; as if I wasn't nervous enough, as soon as I took a seat, she smiled and said, "So, tell me about Kristie."

No time for small talk, huh?

I told her about the girls, my job, and my marriage situation. I explained how Clark and I were finally becoming friends and how great I thought it was.

She interrupted me and said, "Tell me about Kristie. Who is she?"

"I am a mother and a ... um, um, used-to-be wife."

She asked, "What else?"

I had no idea what else. There was a long silence. I could not think of a single word to describe what else I was.

"What are your hobbies?"

Hobbies? Cutting grass was all that came to mind.

When I left that day, she asked me to read Ephesians.

Weird, but okay.

* * *

Once I dove into Ephesians, I quickly understood why she wanted me to read it. It was about our "Who is Kristie?" conversation.

She wanted me to start learning who I am in relation to who God is. I get it. The Bible says if we are Christians, the old version of ourselves has died, and the new has been given. That's our new identity in Christ.

Ephesians 1 says we have been blessed with every spiritual blessing: chosen, adopted, redeemed, forgiven, grace-lavished, and unconditionally loved and accepted. We are pure, blameless, and forgiven.

Through Jesus, we have received the hope of spending eternity with God. When we are in Christ, these aspects of our identity can never be altered by what we do.

This was the complete opposite of what the world and my former therapist had told me.

The more I read, the more confused I became. *Jesus loves me. That's great,* I thought, but I didn't feel loved. *How do I make my heart feel what my head just read? And does God really mean me? Everyone else, maybe, but me?*

My therapist told me that sometimes a gap (sin from our life or lies from the enemy) exists between God and us. This gap can also stem from life experiences, situations, and/or how we allow the world to define us. This gap hinders us from believing these truths and living them out. She said, "To live out the fullness of our identities in Christ, we must determine what keeps us from doing so and then surrender it to God."

"How do we figure that out?" I asked.

"You dig into scripture and start replacing the lies with God's truth."

That simple, huh?

"Start with what you've read in Ephesians that God says you are. Determine which statements you believe are true about you and which aren't."

Being someone who does as she's told with a touch of perfectionism, I went home and dug into my Bible and commentary like a madwoman. I spent hours at my kitchen table with two Bibles, a notebook, several highlighters, and many colored pens. I would highlight every scripture about identity, write it in my notebook along with the commentary, and then pray.

The more I read, the more I learned. I was shocked by how our identity and

Jesus' love go hand in hand for us. I began to understand that I could return to God scarred, broken, and sinful. And sinful I was.

Before long, I started pouring my heart out to God. I hadn't done that in so long because I had never felt he was listening much before, but now I had hope that he was.

Sometimes I prayed for things I didn't even understand I was praying for, so I prayed for understanding. I begged God to reveal the lies that kept me from believing, seeing, and feeling his truth. I prayed that he would help me shed them once he showed me. I prayed for his strength to one day become the woman my therapist told me God created me to be. Oh, how I longed to meet her and to hug her.

My therapist had told me every morning to get up, look directly into the mirror and say, "I am worthy. I am valuable. I am loved. I have a purpose." She said, "No matter how much God has done for us, if we don't believe it, we will never claim it for ourselves."

Not long after that, I began identifying some of the lies I had believed for so long. I believed I was:

- rejected instead of accepted
- in chains instead of set free
- under the law instead of covered by grace
- orphaned instead of adopted

My therapist began to help me to unpack and understand the beliefs behind these lies. Through prayer, God's Word, and the intervention of the Holy Spirit, I began learning about him and his love for me.

* * *

I read about the woman at the well in John 4. My commentary said, "This woman had five husbands and is living with another man, yet she is still lonely." It continued, "That empty place in her heart can only be filled by God, and the same is true for us; only God can quench the deepest thirst of our souls. Nothing else will ever be enough until his love and acceptance are."

My heart started pounding inside my chest. I knew I had also been trying to fill those empty spaces in my heart with other people.

Immediately, I felt the Holy Spirit convicting me, so I prayed.

> God, Take these lies that are holding me in bondage. I don't want
> to believe them anymore. I want to believe what you say about
> me is true. I want to know and feel your truth to live it. I am so

broken, and I've been trying to fix it alone, but I can't. I need you
to come inside my heart and head and take control. I surrender.
I'm tired of trying to do this on my own. I need you; I want you.
I want you to live inside of me. I want to be different; I want to be
changed. Dear Lord, please transform me to desire you the way
you desire me. Take away anything standing between us. Amen.

I wept that night until my body felt empty. I repented and thanked God for continuing to love and pursue me, and I surrendered the rest of my life to him that night.

I fell asleep crying and woke up with a full heart. I felt mended, which I had never felt before. I felt peace within my soul.

Driving to work, I felt God telling me that the relationship I was in needed to end. I knew right then that was what was keeping me separated from him. It was the barrier my therapist had spoken to me about. Deep down, I knew it, but I was desperate to hang on to it because I was afraid to let go and be alone.

That day, I understood how the weight of our sin holds us back and keeps us separated from God. My sin and the lies I believed were the gaps hindering me from fully embracing God and his Word.

Once God opened my eyes to this sin, it showed me how much my life would need to change if I wanted to change. This information convicted me about how I wanted to operate other aspects of my life, from the simplest choices down to my thoughts. And from the tremendous pressure I felt on my soul, I knew this change needed to start immediately, so I ended the relationship I was in.

My therapist was right. With a clearer perspective and a new mindset, I began to understand what Paul was saying in Ephesians: as a Christian, a child of God, my identity and worth came from Christ.

This meant I was free from striving to earn love for my acceptance and value. I didn't need to rely on a man or my girls to fill me up. *I love being a mom, but that isn't what defines me any longer. Being a child of God is what defines me and makes me worthy—and no one gets to redefine what God has already defined.*

*   *   *

I learned independence and self-control.

Everything in my life was changing, and this change felt good. When I looked in a mirror for the first time ever, I smiled back at myself. I liked who I was becoming. I knew this was all because of my reliance on and surrender to God, but I also recognized I still had free will.

Free will meant I had to make choices that weren't easy—and there were some I didn't love—but if they were right and aligned themselves in the direction I needed to go, they had to be made.

Learning about my trauma and discovering my newfound identity helped tremendously in my decision-making process. It also helped me understand why I did the things I did or thought the way I thought; letting others make my decisions had blocked me from knowing myself.

Now, I was making decisions on my own without fear and standing up for them. I wasn't a timid, fearful soul anymore.

Making my own choices introduced me to myself—the girl I had been searching my whole life for. I had finally found her.

It was weird at first. I felt like someone completely new, but, really, I was. I understood that I am a sinner but also forgiven and made new in Christ.

Realizing Jesus loved me and accepted me despite my sin was what permitted me to start loving and valuing myself. This allowed me to start replacing the expectations of others with the thoughts of Jesus, the only one who is truly capable of filling me anyway. This mindset started eliminating the people-pleasing component.

If I am worthy of being loved by God, then I also had to learn to love myself. Receiving God's love meant I needed to love and accept myself because God does. If I mattered to God, then I needed to matter to *me*. I had to create a healthy relationship with myself. The lies I once believed about myself were powerful and self-destructive; they existed because I didn't know the truth. Since I know the truth now, I can't live in fear and insecurity any longer. I must live in truth.

When I learned to live without letting my fears and insecurities dictate my decisions, I realized I could also love without fear. The more I let go of the fear of not performing or pleasing others, the more I valued myself. My chains had been broken, and I was free.

Once I absorbed, processed, and applied all of this to my life, it was like I had permission to be who God had intended me to be. With God's permission and blessing, I became independent and self-confident. I was unstoppable, but it was not in a self-serving way. I was unstoppable with God by my side.

At twenty-eight years old, I finally learned I was an adult who didn't have to explain herself to others and wait for their validation to proceed. This shocked me. Who knew? I slowly implemented these changes in my life to reflect the woman I was becoming:

- I stopped people-pleasing. I started making decisions based on what was right and best for my girls and me—and not what made everyone else happy.

- I stopped apologizing. I am who God made me, and I won't apologize for being too much or not enough for some people.
- I stopped beating myself up for being human. When I don't perform or meet others' expectations, I accept that I'm flawed and will disappoint people occasionally. I'm not perfect, and I don't need to try to attain perfection.
- I stopped asking for permission. I am a grown adult who can make her own decisions. If I want to leave my house at nine o'clock at night because I want to go to Walmart, I can—and I don't need permission to do so.
- I stopped defending myself. I quit explaining and trying to make everyone understand why I did or didn't do something. Whether they know, understand, or think I'm right or wrong doesn't matter.
- I stopped doubting myself. Doubt is from the enemy. I started praying for God to bless or redeem my decisions and left it there.
- I stopped feeling guilty for having needs and wants. My needs and wants don't make me a bad person. They don't make me a needy or high-maintenance person; they represent that I'm human. God gave us the desires of our hearts, and pursuing them is okay.
- I stopped letting others control me or make my decisions. Period. No one gets to tell me what to do anymore. I take ownership of myself and my life. I'm not in control, and I do not need to be controlled.
- I stopped pretending my feelings and opinions didn't matter. My feelings do matter. Even if they only matter to me, they still matter. I shouldn't brush them off or feel silly or insignificant because no one else cares. My opinions are still relevant. I don't have to change them because no one else agrees. I can think and feel for myself. I don't need others to do that for me. I am capable.
- I stopped letting the outside world and those around me dictate, define, or give me value. I started filtering all my decisions, thoughts, and behaviors through God. If my thoughts, behaviors, and decisions align with God's Word and lead me closer to him, then I continue forward. If they don't, I readjust my direction. He is the only one leading me now.

I learned so many things, and they were all so needed. What I mainly learned is that I should have gone to therapy sooner!

*   *   *

Have I not commanded you? Be strong and courageous.
Do not be afraid; do not be discouraged, for the Lord
your God will be with you wherever you go.
—Joshua 1:9

*   *   *

I learned that a healthy marriage isn't one-sided—both of us needed healing.

My first therapist told me that a healthy marriage isn't one-sided. I mulled that one over for weeks, letting the truth sink in: I couldn't save our marriage alone.

But a troubled marriage isn't one-sided either. I finally understood how my wounds kept getting in the way of my marriage, hindering us from moving forward. Those scars were the bumps I kept running into, and they belonged to me—not Clark—and I had to own them to get over them.

I now know every time something bad happened between Clark and me, I would take it personally, try to defend myself, or beat myself up about it—and all that did was irritate those scabs and cause me to bleed onto both of us.

I had to acknowledge that I had allowed my wounds to bleed all over my marriage. I did not intentionally do this, but I still had to take responsibility for it. I had to own my mess in our marriage and quit believing Clark was the only problem. I had to take ownership of my sin instead of saying it was because of someone else's actions.

And I did. I apologized to Clark. He needed to know that I knew he wasn't entirely responsible for our mess, as I had blamed him for many years. I owned my responsibility and shared some of my healing journey with him. I was hopeful that would help him begin to heal.

Even if we couldn't heal our marriage, Clark and I both needed healing, we had wounded each other badly in the first part of our marriage, and no healing had occurred during the second part.

My therapist stressed that neither of us could have a healthy relationship with anyone if we didn't first heal ourselves. I relayed the message to Clark, but he just shrugged. I knew I couldn't force healing upon him, but I would continue pursuing healing and change. I was the only one I could control, and for the first time in my life, I was controlling my own life.

At any rate, my side of the relationship would be as healthy as I individually could be. I was working on myself. It was all I could do, but it was significant.

*   *   *

> "But I will restore you to health and heal
> your wounds," declares the Lord.
> —Jeremiah 30:17

* * *

I learned to listen and follow God's voice.

> For God does speak—now one way, now another—thought no one perceives
> it. In a dream, a vision of the night, when deep sleep falls on people as
> they slumber in their beds, he may speak in their ears and terrify them
> with warnings, to turn them from wrongdoing and keep them from pride,
> to preserve them from the pit, their lives from perishing by the sword.
> —Job 33:14–18

* * *

I never used to hear God because I was so busy running. I would not allow myself to get still long enough to hear him, much less listen to what he was saying. I couldn't think about anything beyond myself. It was all about me, my feelings, my wants, and my needs. I wouldn't slow down long enough to ask God what he wanted.

Honestly, I didn't know God wanted me to ask him things like that. I accepted Jesus at a young age, but I had never been discipled or taken the time to form a personal relationship with him. All I knew before this separation started was to read my Bible for biblical knowledge. I have now learned that biblical wisdom is sound, but it's the application of the information that leads to transformation. A relationship with Jesus is way more important than being able to spew off biblical knowledge, but don't let me get ahead.

One night right after I left Clark, as I was about to fall asleep, I heard God whisper, "Come back to me." I remember feeling so scared. Surely, God wasn't asking me to return after what I had done. Fearful of the God I thought I knew, I prayed what I thought he wanted to hear. "God, I will come back. I've made such a mess of things that I'm too ashamed right now, but I am working on it. I promise I'll fix them and make them right, and I'll be back. I will make you proud."

A month or so into this journey of reading Ephesians, meeting weekly with my new therapist, and doing a lot of work to understand how me, my identity, and Jesus fit together, I heard that same voice again: "Come back to me." Immediately, I knew it was God talking to me, and this time, I wasn't fearful.

My heart felt it; God was calling me back into a relationship with him because I had been running.

I had no idea that I had been running from God the time before. I knew nothing about a true relationship with him. I knew and believed in him, but I had no idea that he was all I needed, that he would be the one to heal me, or that there was nothing I could do to make myself good enough for him. I wish I did—it could have saved me a lot of heartache—but I didn't. Instead, I thought, *I must make myself all those things before returning to him.* God is so good, and he will wait. He will meet us right where we are if we allow him to.

The day God asked me to end the relationship I was in was the day my transformation began. Once I heard him, I knew I had to obey. There was no turning back; otherwise, I would never be able to grow into the woman I had prayed to become. I couldn't keep praying for something if I wasn't willing to put in the work.

That day, I chose to enter into a different relationship with God. I entered with a pure heart, seeking to know and do his will over mine, and out of this, I found myself in pursuit of him. I found myself clinging to him—and not just in times of brokenness. I learned about the strength that I can have only through him.

I found myself leaning into God's truth differently. The more I learned, the more I was able to listen. The more I listened, the more I could hear. Hearing more gave me the courage and the desire to continue following.

This was where I began growing in God. Growing in God felt much better than growing in myself, as my old therapist had been trying to teach me.

* * *

Consequently, faith comes from hearing the message, and
the message is heard through the word about Christ.
—Romans 10:17

* * *

But let me be clear, just because I learned this doesn't mean everything got nice and easy, and Jesus and I lived happily ever after. No, that won't happen until I meet him in eternity. On this side of heaven, the enemy is still lurking, waiting to devour us like prey.

I was in the very early stages of this transformation, and it was tough to make a break from that guy. It took every bit of self-control (I did not have) not to call him or see him.

Did I mess up? You bet I did. Remember the free will thing? But the Holy Spirit convicted me of my choices. Staying connected to the Holy Spirit and pursuing Jesus allowed me to hear him. I learned that I had to depend on God for his strength and not mine during times like this because my strength would fail me every time.

I had to return to my knees and pray for the Lord to intervene, sometimes several times a day. Every time I asked, though, he provided. He would guide and redirect my thoughts and my steps.

Being aware of the spirit working inside of me reassured me that I was changing and growing. Knowing Jesus better gave me grace for myself because grace comes from Jesus. Knowing Jesus forgave me didn't permit me to keep messing up; it held me to a higher level of accountability.

As I talked to my therapist about this, she suggested I take time out from dating and get to know myself more. Even though dating wasn't technically a sin, things were still cloudy for me. I was in the thick of learning, growing, and changing; it was a process I needed to evolve into with only myself and the Lord.

She showed me how I went from a dictator-style parent home straight into being a parent myself, to marriage, separation, and now into another relationship. I had no time alone or on my own.

She also challenged me to grow in my spiritual discipline. Since I had no idea what spiritual discipline meant, she gave me four principles to implicate into my daily routine:

1. Bible time. Not a day should go by without reading the Bible, even if it is for ten minutes a day.
2. Bible study. We need to be involved in Bible study. Don't get Bible time and Bible study confused. Bible time involves the Lord and you. Bible study is about growing, digging deeper, and being in a community.
3. Solitude. Solitude is a must, even if it's once a week. We all must talk less and listen more.
4. Prayer. Prayer is essential. Pray as if you are talking to your best friend. It doesn't have to be formal. No matter what you say to God, it's never wrong. He knows our hearts, and we must not worry about praying wrong. Just pray—and pray about everything. This grows our relationship with him.

I had to face the sin and distractions of my life and get still before the Lord to hear him. Allowing myself to get quiet and still before the Lord with all the truth I had learned allowed me to see how desperate I was for satisfaction. I had been in an endless cycle of seeking and searching in all the wrong places.

Allowing myself to get quiet and still before the Lord revealed my sin, the distractions, and all the fears I had been avoiding. Suddenly, I wasn't afraid anymore because I could feel God's presence with me, and I felt brave enough to tackle them with truth instead of running.

Allowing myself to get quiet and still before the Lord showed me the difference between quietness and loneliness. It wasn't the quietness that bothered me before; it was the loneliness. I didn't know who I was, so I tried to escape her.

Those spiritual disciplines became an essential part of my life, and that is where my relationship with God became intimate, my faith grew, and my focus on the law began to diminish. Growing in God's Word *and* having a personal relationship with him changed everything I knew about my life.

I now take time for myself, invest in me, listen to me, get to know me better, and spend time with me. Me alone and me lonely—those are two different girls.

Allowing myself to get quiet and still before the Lord created a relationship between the Lord and me, and when he speaks now, I hear him and am not afraid. I'm hopeful.

* * *

And so we know and rely on the love God has for us. God is love. Whoever lives in love lives in God, and God in them.
—1 John 4:16

* * *

But the ultimate test in hearing and obeying God's voice lay just ahead …

P A R T

III

RECONSTRUCTING

CHAPTER 8

TRUSTING GOD'S PROMISES

My sheep listen to my voice; I know them, and they follow Me.
—John 10:27

I woke up around midnight and heard someone calling my name. I quickly remembered it wasn't my night with the girls. That was so strange; I swear I heard someone calling my name.

I lay back down somewhere between being scared for my life and curious about whether I was dreaming. As I lay there, wide-awake, a faint voice said, "Go home."

Go home? I thought. *I must be dreaming.*

I closed my eyes.

"Go home."

I heard it again? Who is here?

"Go home."

"I am home," I blurted out. *That was silly, Kristie.*

I heard the voice louder: "Go home."

I sat up in bed, trying to wrap my head around this. *Am I dreaming?*

"Go home."

I heard that voice, and I was scared. My heart started pounding. I was breathing hard, almost in tears, and shaking. I was still not sure what was happening.

"God, is that you?"

"Go home."

Why would I go home? Clark doesn't want me, and I don't want to be there."

"Go home."

"Why do you want me to go home?"

This was so bizarre. I couldn't even comprehend why he would say this. I felt like I had come to a place where I knew when God was talking versus the enemy. I knew this was God, but it made no sense.

"Go home."

"You want me to go home?"

"Go home."

"To Clark?"

"Go home."

"To *that* marriage?"

"Go home."

"I don't understand."

"Go home."

This is absurd. I'm going back to sleep. "God, we can talk about this tomorrow."

"Go home."

I could not shake this voice. I was trying hard to ignore it. My heart was still beating rapidly, and the longer I lay there, the harder it became to breathe. *Am I having a heart attack? Seriously, my hands feel numb and tingly.*

I got up to get some water, but I fell.

Breathe, Kristie. Breathe. I started taking deep breaths until I finally felt my heart rate slowing down. I stood back up and immediately heard the voice again: "Go home."

"But God—"

"Go home!"

My heart rate sped up again. I was not dreaming. I was awake. Without thinking, I grabbed my phone and keys, and out the door I went. It all happened so fast; I was on the interstate before I realized what was happening. I was aware that God was talking to me, and I feared what might have happened if I had not gotten up and left. I remembered that I had promised to be obedient, and as much as I did not like it or understand it, he was asking me to go. He was asking me to trust him.

It's a wonder I didn't get in a wreck. All of a sudden, I thought, *What in the world am I going to do? Am I just going to knock on the door and say, "Hey, honey, I'm home"?* That's when the panic set in again.

I made it to his road and thought I was about to start hyperventilating. I pulled over, and I sat there for thirty minutes, trying to calm down and think.

I started talking to God. "Why would you want me to go home? I don't understand why you would ask me to do this."

I still can't let it go, even though I know that's how we humans are. We think if we know the answer, then being obedient will be much easier, but that is not true. God only allows us to know one step at a time because knowing his full will would overwhelm us, and we would never get off the first step. And obeying that first step is faith in him. Trusting that what he's calling us to do is good and right and better than we could imagine.

Silence.

"God, I have changed. I am a different person. Why would you want me to go back home? Why would you do that to me? I don't understand."

Still silence.

"God, where are you? Talk to me!" *Maybe I heard him wrong.* As quickly as that thought came to my mind, I knew I did not hear him wrong. I prayed, "God, I am sorry. Help me to trust you … help my unbelief."

At that moment, I heard God say, "Trust me. I will resurrect your marriage. I will make it even better than you could imagine."

I giggled and thought, *Let's not get ahead of ourselves here,* but I felt his presence and knew he was not kidding.

I felt a peace come upon me, and I drove up to the house. I pulled into the driveway and called Clark and asked him to open the door. I had no idea what would happen, but I knew what I had to do. *Sink or swim,* I thought. *God is in control, and I am not.*

The light came on. As I walked along the sidewalk, I prayed, "Dear Lord, catch me when I fall."

The door opened, and there stood Clark. He looked half asleep and baffled. "Is everything okay? Are you okay? What … what are you doing here?"

I couldn't bring myself to look at him.

"Kristie, what are you doing here?"

Startled, I looked up and caught his eyes. "I don't know!"

He rolled his eyes, and he cocked his head. "You don't know why you are here at two thirty in the morning?"

With tears rolling down my cheek, I said, "God told me to come home."

He said nothing.

I muttered, "I'm sorry. I know this was a bad idea."

Clark stepped back, opened the door wider, and said, "What took you so long?"

*   *   *

Doing what God called you to do, I found out, doesn't always feel good at the time. Five weeks in, with my bags packed, I called my friend to tell her it was a mistake—and I was leaving. I knew she would understand because she was the one who told me I was a fool to go back.

Instead, she reminded me that we are called to be obedient to God.

"What do you mean?" I knew what she meant. I was hoping for a loophole.

"Kristie, I don't know if I necessarily believe God called you back to this marriage. Personally, I thought it was a hot mess, but I know you believe that God called you back to this marriage, and if you believe that, then you must obey."

Faintly I said, "I should," unsure if that was a question or a comment.

"So ... do you believe God called you back ... or that it's a mistake?"

"God called me back."

"Then you don't get to leave because the feelings you had the other night have left. If you believe what you say you do, you have to stay. You must remain committed—even when the hard parts come and the good feelings leave. That's what obedience is: staying committed to what God has called you to do despite the conditions."

I started crying.

"What's wrong?" she asked.

"I thought you would understand."

"No, you thought I would give you permission to leave."

I giggled. She was right.

"If this is where God has called you, and you don't feel at peace about it right now, then pray about it."

> God, If I believe your promise, why does it feel like we are still broken? If you wanted me to come home, why are things still so complex and confusing, like our feelings? And what are our feelings? Doesn't this automatically mean we love each other because I'm back?
>
> I feel like he loves me, but it's different than I've ever experienced with him, and it scares me. It scares me because it feels genuine and compassionate. I catch him looking at me with a smile and a weird glare in his eyes. It makes my heart feel good, but it makes me extremely uncomfortable at the same time. I've never felt this from him. I'm afraid it won't last, and, God, I'm afraid that it will.
>
> God, What is love? What does it look like and feel like? I mean, I do love Clark. I don't know if I love him like a wife should love her husband. I don't glare and smile at him like he does me. God, I am here because you asked me to come home, and I know I need to be obedient after everything I have learned, but I am so confused right now. I assumed that if I were obedient, things would be easier than this. I thought you rewarded obedience. I thought you would fix everything and

restore the feelings. This thing is, God, everything isn't fixed; in fact, nothing is fixed. Everything is complicated, weird, awkward, and uneasy. It's like we're walking on eggshells.

God, I don't know what your plan is, and I don't know what I'm supposed to do. I don't even know if I want to be here, but what I do know is that I trust you. You have brought me so far this past year—you have led me, healed me, and changed me—so I'm committed to staying. I'm not going anywhere, but I need you to change my heart. Give me the desire to be here, God, and help us find our way back to each other— not like before but better, as you promised. I'm holding you to that promise, God.

God, show me what I need to do. Help me, lead me, give me patience, and take away these feelings of anxiousness. Amen.

Immediately after I closed my journal, I heard the Lord ask, "Dear child, do you trust me?"

"Yes, Lord. I trust you," I said with a smile.

"Then abide in me, and I will you."

* * *

Three months in, the house dynamics were going well. Maybe so well that I was skeptical that they would stay this way. I felt like I was living with a totally different Clark. This new version of Clark asked about my day, offered to babysit, and gave me time alone. He even walked around the neighborhood with me while the kids rode their bikes and held my hand.

Clark wasn't just present now; he was attentive to all of us. He participated in daily activities and events inside and outside the home, and he seemed to enjoy it.

Watching him become a hands-on dad won my heart the most. It gave me so much hope, and I was so encouraged by the changes I saw in Clark.

I loved how things were going, but subconsciously I was waiting for the ball to drop. I think that's why I proceeded so cautiously with loving him.

Remaining cautious about what I knew was God's plan positioned me back to listening to my feelings instead of trusting God's promise.

My feelings told me we could never make this marriage work. They reminded me of how many times we had tried before and failed. They told me that if Clark knew everything I had done while we were apart, he wouldn't want me back, which made me question the same about him.

My feelings told me this was too hard; we would never be able to forget our hurts and move past them, we'd never be able to create a new marriage, and we'd be better off starting over with someone new who we didn't have all the past hurt and pain to carry with us and try to navigate through. My feelings were fears that told me Clark would never be able to love me, and it would be best to end things before we got too deep.

My feelings contradicted everything God had promised me.

I prayed about this, and a few weeks later, I heard God's voice, "My child, you are leaning too much on your feelings and not on my truth. When you do that, you allow the enemy to occupy space in your head. You have to take every thought captive to prevent this."

As I prayed more about this, God reminded me to slow my thoughts and remember his promise. He reassured me that worrying about whether Clark could love me was an old toxic way of thinking and not to allow that lie to occupy any headspace. I understood through therapy how I had moved past that, and reverting back could stunt the growth I had made or hinder future growth.

God told me to examine when the enemy was talking versus him. The enemy delivers fear and worry—not God. God had a plan. He sent me home; he was in control. He loved me, and he would protect me. I could trust that.

God calmed my heart, allowing me to stand upon the truth I've learned and cling to his promises. I knew this, but sometimes I got so worked up that I couldn't think clearly.

That's why being still and returning to prayer is so important. I heard him say, "Seek me when you are feeling scared or afraid. It is only I who can fill you anyway. It is only I who can give you what you need. Clark's love will be a bonus, but it is I who will sustain you."

I realized right then that my dependence on God would be what sustains me through every other relationship in life. I needed God. I had to depend on him; there was no other choice.

* * *

We demolish arguments and every pretension that sets
itself up against the knowledge of God, and we take captive
every thought to make it obedient to Christ.
—2 Corinthians 10:5

* * *

Clark and I were so good at avoiding hard conversations and pretending. I hated hard conversations, especially when I had to talk about myself and how I felt. Letting someone into the deepest parts of me feels scary. To admit my fears and insecurities, umm, no thanks, but I knew it was time.

I remembered the last time Clark and I tried to jump back in and pretend nothing ever happened. I didn't want to make that mistake again.

I knew going forward, my feelings must be shared with Clark—and not just processed and filtered through my head, forming my own conclusions. He deserved to know how I was feeling, and he deserved the opportunity to respond with his truth. Knowing his truth would be much better than creating his conclusions to my thoughts anyway.

I had to be brave and use the vulnerability skills I had learned to avoid repeating those past mistakes. I also had to put my newfound trust in God in action and open myself up to Clark, even if it left me vulnerable or exposed.

Feeling more confident in God's truth and promise, I felt ready to take this bold step forward in faith and obedience. I arranged a night out for us, without the children, and I planned on talking to him about my feelings and fears, and my hopes and dreams.

But first, I prayed.

> Dear Lord, help me seek your will today and give me the strength to endure it. Give me the strength to stand here and wait upon you. Give me the strength to be brave and talk to Clark about my feelings. Give him the same strength to talk back. Break down all the barriers that the enemy is trying to keep up. Bridge this gap between us, Lord. Fix what's broken in us and allow us to lean into you and your truths—not our own. Prepare my heart to show Clark the same love you have shown me. Amen

*   *   *

And then I wrote a note.

> Dear Clark,
>
> I planned a night out for us tonight. I have so much confusion going on inside my head and heart. I want to be honest about how I'm feeling. I want us to navigate this together instead of

trying to do it our way like all the other times before. That didn't work, so I believe we must take a different route this time if we want different results. I have no idea how to fix this marriage or put it back together, but I believe God does. I want to let him give us instructions on how he wants us to navigate this. I don't know if that makes sense to you, but it feels like the right way to me. I can try to explain what I mean by this tonight if you need me to.

So please use today to think about any questions or anything you want to say. God called me back to you, to this marriage; I know you know this, so understand that tonight won't be about accusing, proving points, or about who's right or wrong. This will be a safe space where we invite God to be a part of us and ask the enemy to leave, so please come knowing that you won't be attacked or criticized, or told you are wrong for your thoughts and feelings. I know I was notorious for those things in the past, but I'm not that person anymore. God has been working within me, so please redirect me if I go in that direction.

I am both excited and scared of this talk, but I am willing to have hard conversations and do hard things when God leads me to them now, no matter the cost.

Love,
Kristie

On the way to dinner, I asked God, "How do I learn to love Clark as I have you?"

"The same way you came to love me. Spend time with him. Get to know him. Focus on the things he does instead of the things he doesn't. Be patient and wait."

God's words were exactly what I needed to hear right then. They calmed my heart and changed my perspective.

At dinner, I told Clark, "God is giving us a second chance, so let's start over and relearn each other. Let's pretend this is our first date—and we're getting to know each other. I mean, we'll go home and take care of the same kids later, but tonight, right now, let's start over."

He smirked and said, "Hey, I'm Clark, and I'm in love with a girl named Kristie, and if she catches me with you, she will go nuts."

I giggled. "I'm Kristie, and I love with a boy named Clark, whom I fear will break my heart again, so I'm afraid to go all in.

"That boy is a man now, and he's not going to hurt you. Take all the time you need because he's not going anywhere."

"Good … because I don't want him to."

*   *   *

Clark and I needed that night. It was beautiful and so much fun; we joked, laughed, and talked the entire time. It brought me back to us and made me want more. However, I knew life wouldn't always be like that night. I knew we would need something more to sustain us daily for survival. My therapist had talked about sustainability and how it took deep roots to cultivate and grow. I didn't know how to 'plant' us, but I knew who did.

Guess who finally showed up to therapy with me? When Clark walked through my therapist's door, her face lit up, and the sweetest smile emerged. I knew we were going to be okay. It was my godwink.

Out of that, and over time, we made some new rules and agreements.

The major one is that divorce is not an option. We promised each other that divorce is not an option—no matter how hard things get. It's amazing how differently you argue or work toward a resolution when you know you have to compromise, find a middle ground, or live miserably because there are no other options. And who wants to live miserably? Not me anymore.

Since divorce isn't an option, it made me feel like we are finally on the same team. When conflicts or hurt feelings arise, your perspective differs because you know you are working toward the same goal. All teams have the same goal in mind, and that is to win. We both want our marriage to win. There is no giving up when you are part of a team.

On our team, we established that there are no assigned positions; you do what is needed for the team's sake. Sometimes, oftentimes, it requires filling in the gap for the other person.

The second rule is that all decisions we make in our marriage must be God-honoring ones. If they wouldn't honor God, don't make them. We honor God with our choices, decisions, thoughts, and actions—no ifs, ands, or buts about it.

We also changed some specific behaviors. We started getting the kids to bed together, and then we went to bed at the same time. We have nightly check-ins, even if it's just five minutes, and weekly date nights. We talk to listen and understand rather than to be right.

Clark began eating lunch with me daily, taking a full hour off work and bringing me lunch. He'd never done that before, and I loved it. We talked, we laughed, and we checked in with each other during the day. We took the kids on walks and to the park and did family things together. No more "me and the kids" and "him."

We went to church and found a group to be a part of. We understood that community was vital. We pray together, which opened up vulnerability real quick!

Clark and I set up vulnerability nights one night a week where we got to ask anything we desired to know about the other, and the other person had to answer as vulnerably as possible.

When we first implemented these changes, it felt like we were checking boxes. The feelings didn't return all at once, but it felt good to finally have a teammate.

God reminded me it takes time to heal and put back together what was broken.

I knew without a doubt that I was supposed to be there. I didn't understand why, but I knew God had called me home. The fact that Clark let me come home with no questions asked was proof that God had been preparing Clark's heart for this as well.

I held fast to God's promises and believed he would restore my marriage with all my heart. I quit trying to imagine what that marriage would look like because God told me that wasn't the point. He convicted me that I needed to stay focused on him and start leaning fully into the marriage he had sent me home to. He told me to start living as if the promises had already been delivered and to stop responding to all the different emotions and acting differently depending on them.

God blessed me, though, and as I clung to him, he never let me down. I always felt his presence and strength to keep going, especially during this weird waiting period of my return home.

*   *   *

A few months later, I could feel the tide changing. It was shifting. My heart felt a little different. I couldn't quite explain it. More smiles. More hugs. More talk. More peace. More freedom.

I found myself getting excited around the time he would come home. *This is new,* I thought. But I liked it, and I wanted to keep it.

I knew this change inside of me didn't come from Clark. It wasn't something I had learned recently; it was a complete change from the inside.

God had become my sense of source, and he became my best friend, the one my true soul desired.

*   *   *

For in this hope we were saved. But hope that is seen is no hope
at all. Who hopes for what they already have? But if we hope
for what we do not yet have, we wait for it patiently.
—Romans 8:24–25

*   *   *

CHAPTER 9

REBUILDING IS HARDER
THAN STAYING BROKEN

We were getting ready for church on Mother's Day, and the girls were so excited for me to open their gifts. They came bursting through my bedroom door: "Mommy, Mommy, open our gifts! We made it, especially for you! Daddy helped us!"

Clark knows how much I adore my children's artwork or anything handmade by them. I tore off the wrapping paper and found a scrapbook. I love making scrapbooks, but I never thought I'd see the day Clark made a scrapbook! As I turned page after page, I could tell much time and effort had been put into it.

Picture after picture, page after page of our past, had a fun, special memory written beside it. However, I didn't remember those fun memories in the way he described them. I saw the family picture with Mickey Mouse that we stood in line for an hour to get while arguing about him going out drinking the night before with my dad.

I saw the Key West photo and remembered arguing so horribly on the cruise that our friends were uncomfortable.

I saw the five of us standing under the Carowinds sign and remembered how we barely talked that weekend.

And then I saw it—the ultrasound picture of when there were two babies—and I instantly remembered how he left me. All that pain, hurt, disappointment, bitterness, and resentment immediately filled my mind. All I saw in that scrapbook was heartache and things I had been trying to forget for the past six months.

Why would he do this? All I can see, feel, and remember is pain. Does he not see it or remember it the way I do? Why highlight the very thing I've been trying to stuff?

The girls and Clark stared at me as tears ran down my face. I mumbled, "I love it," but my heart was aching. I was home and wanted to make new memories, ones that didn't break my heart and make me cry. I longed for days of pictures when I could look at them, smile, and say, "Remember this?"

Will Clark and I ever have those? Will we ever get there? Or have I just been pretending again? Hoping? I said nothing to Clark about how I felt; instead, I lied and said, "I love it."

Lying and stuffing my feelings was a pattern from the past that I did not want to start remaking. First thing on Monday morning, I called my therapist, and by some miracle, she was able to see me that day. Just sitting in the waiting room had me all worked up. When she called my name, I burst through her door. "You are not going to believe what happened!"

"What's going on today, Kristie?"

I started talking a mile a minute. No breaths—just ranting and complaining.

"Slow down. Breathe. Take me back to the start and tell me about this scrapbook."

"It's like a through-the-years scrapbook. It starts with Katelyn. It has tons of pictures of us, and it talks about how he saw me with her, and then goes to Kelsey and the same thing, and then to Brooke. The next pages are pictures of all of us through the past ten years, and he has little happy memories written beside them—except they aren't happy memories. They are painful memories that I try not to think about. His words are so kind and sweet. But if he didn't mean them then, how can he mean them now? Maybe now that he's looking back, he can see it, but back then, he didn't care what kind of mother I was."

"When an experience is recorded as a memory, it goes through the emotional and cognitive filters, assumptions, and interpretations of the person."

"Huh?"

"Clark may not think of those memories as painful as you do."

"How? It's the truth! Those things did happen."

"The emotional charge of a memory comes mostly from the stories we tell ourselves about a difficult experience. It's the emotional charge of a memory that makes it so potent."

"I need some more explanation."

"That's why two people can tell the same story in two different ways. The facts are the same, but the feelings behind the story are different."

So my feelings aren't always right? That seems so wrong to me. I feel this way because of what happened. How does that make me wrong?

As she began to speak, feeling like she was about to defend him, I cut her off.

"Well, you won't believe what was on the last page! The last page had an ultrasound picture of the baby that died, and he wrote about that too." By this time, my tears were falling like raindrops.

"Kristie, do you think the scrapbook would have been so hurtful if he omitted the ultrasound picture?"

"Probably. But just a little," I said.

"Why does visually seeing the past hurt you, Kristie?"

"It reminds me of who we were." .

"But you and Clark aren't those same people anymore."

"I know." I smiled. "We aren't." That thought made me happy.

"What's the difference between seeing the past and remembering the past?"

"I don't feel the past. I avoid all those thoughts and feelings."

"How?"

"I don't think about them. If something takes me there, I go somewhere else in my mind or redirect myself physically. I stay busy."

"Kristie, it's time."

"For what?"

"To heal from the first ten years of your marriage."

"I thought I did."

"You healed from your childhood."

"I have to heal from my childhood *and* my marriage?"

"Kristie, you've processed your childhood, grown spiritually, and entered back into your marriage, but you haven't healed the hurt that it inflicted upon you. And Clark probably hasn't either."

"Sometimes, I think it would be easier to start all over." *I can't believe I said that out loud. I've certainly thought about it before. One or two times—maybe ten. It's true, though; building on a new foundation sounded easier than building on a broken one.*

"Isn't that what y'all are doing?"

"I mean with different people. With no memories. From scratch and with no pain. Fresh."

"Do you think things would be better that way?"

"It would be easier."

"Do you want easy?"

I give her a half smile. "Easy doesn't sound too bad right now."

"The old Kristie wanted easy, but if the new Kristie were interested in easy, she wouldn't have gone back to a broken marriage."

I thought about her words.

"These past six months haven't been easy, but you have stayed committed because of your faith and obedience to God. Kristie, you have changed, and this change has brought tremendous growth. What you are doing is extremely brave. Don't run now. God has brought you here and allowed everything that has happened to lead you to this moment."

"So what now?"

"Quit running and trying to avoid your painful past. Do the work it takes to heal."

"I thought I was."

"Because God is at work in you, he wants to help you heal all your pain. He wants to have control of the parts of you that the enemy keeps messing with. The enemy will stop at nothing; he will go as deep as he can to hurt you, confuse you, and make you doubt the good. Make no mistake, the enemy only comes to kill, steal, and destroy, and that's what he is trying to do right now. You can't skip over this part or avoid it; you must deal with it to heal from it. Remember, Kristie, your past controls every part of your future."

"So … is what I've been doing wrong?"

"No, no, no. Don't think that. Don't discard the growth that has occurred because we wouldn't be here today without any of it. God allows everything to happen in the order it needs to. Our faith and growth build upon each other and strengthen us for the next season of life."

I heard what she said and wondered if this was where God wanted me. Did God have to break me again so I would listen? I thought I had been listening.

She continued, "You have always thought healing meant moving forward on a clean slate and ignoring the hurt, hoping it would go away, but that's not healing. That's just moving forward—still broken. If you want true healing and restoration, you must face your past hurts and regain its power, just like your childhood. I think you are ready now."

"You say that like it's easy!"

"Philippians 4:13 says, 'I can do all things through Christ who strengthens me.' Kristie, you've grown and matured and found your faith in the one true healer, and he thinks you are ready to start understanding what has happened in the past ten years of your marriage. Figure it out so you can learn from it, allow God to use it, to use you, and finally be set free."

It's true. I had grown. I wasn't the same person I was a year ago. *God is my best friend. I know he wants good for me. I trust him. I trust him more than I trust myself. I have to believe he allowed this to happen for my good.*

"Kristie, you keep saying God wants you in this marriage. If that is true, he wouldn't ask you to rebuild over the bumps if he didn't plan on being the builder. If you want the healing, you've got to open yourself up to the healer, and you can't keep any part from him."

I giggled through all the snot and tears and said, "I feel like I've heard this before."

"Several times."

As I stood up to leave, she said, "Rebuilding with bumps and scars is very hard, often difficult. Most couples don't choose to rebuild, or they quit halfway through. That's why divorce rates are so high. Rebuilding a marriage requires a lot of work, sacrifice, and dedication from both sides. It will ask more of you than either can deliver, and that's the part where most people quit. But the secret is, when you get to that part, you let go and let God take control. Draw from his strength. He will deliver. He always does. Don't fear it or fight it—embrace it."

> Rebuilding a marriage requires a lot of hard work, sacrifice, and dedication from both sides. It's going to ask more of you than either can deliver, and that's the part where most people quit. But the secret is, when you get to that part, you let go and let God take control. Draw from his strength. He will deliver.

* * *

I thought rebuilding without Clark would help me avoid all the hurt I had deep inside me, but I realized Clark wasn't the hurt; I was the hurt.

I was broken and afraid of the healing process, so I tried to hang on to control, thinking it would prevent me from breaking. But I was already broken; I didn't understand it completely until now.

The last year, God has slowed me down long enough to feel the uneasiness in my body, and at first, I didn't like it. I wanted to cover it up, make it stop, and ignore it until it hit me smack dab in the face one night; I was running from God!

I was fighting the breaking process because I was afraid if I allowed myself to fall apart and let God put me back together, he might not do it correctly. The way I wanted.

The truth is, I knew I was broken and had control issues. I believed in God and trusted him as long as I got a vote, but I was afraid to allow God's will in my life because I thought I would live a mediocre, half-satisfied, half-filled life. I did that for the past ten years of my life and just wasn't interested anymore.

And then, I met Jesus. Oh, sweet Jesus. As I surrendered, God began stripping away some of the lies I once lived by, and he began replacing them with the truth, his truth.

Learning God and his Word taught me that trust begins with the truth. God's promises are true—he doesn't lie.

There is one therapeutic truth I learned from my childhood healing journey that I applied to my marriage a few months ago that took on a whole new meaning today after therapy: understanding the victim's role.

I understood loud and clear the first time my therapist told me victims either become victors or stay victims and bleed all over everyone they come in contact with. I established early on in therapy that I would no longer be bleeding onto others.

Yes, I know I have been a victim for parts of my life, but I learned I couldn't grow as long as I stayed in a victim mentality, so I worked hard at reshaping my mentality.

This year, I worked hard on growing and not bleeding onto others; I thought I had done well. I am proud of myself and happy with the growth that I achieved.

However, I didn't realize that entering back into a relationship still broken would cause continual bleeding. I also didn't know that I am still broken.

Perhaps, we're always going to remain a little broken.

So here I am again, trying to put myself back together, but I'm not alone. Nor am I attempting to go at it alone. I'm not scared this time because I know I'm not starting from scratch; I'm starting with experience.

I started this rebuilding process a year ago and believe this is just part of my journey.

I have no reason to run or fear this continued rebuilding; all I need to do is embrace it and use the tools I have acquired. I'll remain in God's truth, love, and grace to continue healing. I'll work the steps just like I did the first time and allow God the freedom to move.

He did it once; I have no doubt he will do it again.

What blows my mind is I thought breaking was the hard part. I think that's why I held on for so long, but I now believe breaking is the easy part, and healing is the hard part.

We live in a broken world; why would we think it was hard? It's the fast part; it happens before we even notice. That's how the enemy works. Brokenness stems from the enemy, but we don't have to live broken alone.

This is where my hope comes from: the truth that I don't have to live broken alone. This is why I'm not afraid of doing the work it takes to heal.

I'm not even afraid of breaking anymore, and there is so much freedom in that. Thank you, God.

Rebuilding from brokenness is hard though, and it takes strength and courage that I can't produce alone. But I think that's the point: in order to heal, I must be present with the healer.

I'm here, Lord; I'm here. And I know you're right beside me.

*　*　*

During this season of working on me and my marriage, I was driving and felt the Lord speaking to me: "Dear child, this work is hard, I know, but peace will come from it. Rebuilding this way, with all the bumps and the scars, will make you so much stronger, and you will know it is I who rebuilt you."

I thought back to the earlier days of therapy when I felt like a growing lost puppy. I remember my therapist confronting me and saying, "To put those scars to rest, you must face them until they don't scare you anymore—until they don't have that power over you. That triggering power I spoke about. Right now, it owns you; you can't bury something you don't own."

I felt myself smile and thought, *God, I'm not scared anymore. Those lies don't own me, and the enemy doesn't control me. In fact, he should fear me because I will speak your words right back to him. I'm ready, God, I'm really ready. Let's finish what you've started in me. Change me. Heal me. Transform me. I want to be used for you.*

Allowing God to break and rebuild me was the first step in my restoration journey. Allowing God to continue healing me was the next step in aiding God to heal my marriage.

*　*　*

Search me, God, and know my heart; test me and know
my anxious thoughts. See if there be any offensive way
in me, and lead me in the way everlasting.
—Psalm 139:23–24

*　*　*

One day, my dad showed up at my house unannounced, which shocked me because it had been quite a while since we'd spoken. Clark and I knew it wouldn't go well; it never did.

Before I opened the door, my dad barged in.

"Excuse me," I said in a sarcastic tone.

"Where are the girls?"

"Outside with Clark."

"I came to see the girls. I haven't seen them in months."

"We are getting ready to leave. Maybe another time."

"I don't want to see them another time. I want to see them right now."

I could feel the anger rising inside me, but I had vowed never to let him dictate my emotions or behavior again. Instead, I prayed: "God, help me. I need you to intervene."

"Not today."

My dad started hollering, cussing me so loud that I couldn't hear anything he was saying. I stood there, trying to control my behavior and words because I wanted to respond—not how I knew God wanted me to respond.

As I stood there, I could feel God's hand over my mouth, and at that moment, Clark walked in and said, "Enough. That's enough! Time for you to leave."

"My dad laughed in his face and said, "Boy, do you know who you are talking to?"

"Do you know who you're talking to? That's your daughter you keep disrespecting, and that's my wife. Now it's time to go."

"I'm not going any *blankety-blank* place until I see the girls."

Calmly, Clark said, "Look, today is not a good day, but we will let you see them."

"I'm not going anywhere until I see my girls."

"Darrell, you are not seeing the girls today. Call me, and we will plan a better day. I will ask you again to leave our house before I call the police. You can choose, but you only have ten seconds to decide."

Based on past experiences, I knew we would have to call the police. I was so sure I had already gotten the phone, but instead, my dad turned and walked out the door. *What in the world just happened?*

Clark had just taken control of the situation like a man. Like the head of the house. Like the head of *our* home and family. I saw the protector emerge in him, something I had *never* witnessed before.

I had never seen Clark stand up to my dad or really to anyone. Clark is a man of few words, and confrontation is not his strong point. It's not because he's a coward, but if someone takes Clark to an emotional point like my dad regularly did to me, he would walk away. Clark doesn't deal with things in the moment, especially moments of anger; he lets them cool down and revisits them later. He's a thinker and a processor—not a reactor like me.

Clark had just responded like a man who loved and respected his wife. Like a man who wasn't allowing his wife to fight her battles alone. Like a man who said, "My wife is too valuable to me to let you disrespect her. You've got to leave." I felt like we had just defeated a giant. It was a major victory, and we had done it together.

Chaos was breaking out around me, but I just smiled. Standing before me was the man I had waited for the past ten years of my life for. He had finally arrived. The new and improved version—put back together by God himself.

*   *   *

The Spirit of the Sovereign Lord is on me, because the Lord
has anointed me to proclaim good news to the poor. He has
sent me to bind up the brokenhearted, to proclaim freedom for
the captives and release from darkness for the prisoners.
—Isaiah 61:1

*   *   *

When I returned home, I didn't realize that God had changed Clark too. Maybe you've heard the saying, "God will change the situation—or he'll change you?" Well, I thought God had called me back and would change my heart, but not much else. And that was okay; I agreed to that.

At the time, I did not know the bigness of God and what mighty things he could do. I had faith, but it was small. Faith is like a muscle—the more you use it, the stronger it gets.

I was still learning so much about God and me, and Clark was too. Clark had totally changed. I mean, like to-the-core changed. His heart was different. I think he had a heart transplant too!

I found a notebook where he had been journaling, praying, and even writing poems. *Who is this man?* I was curious and desperately wanted to read them, but I needed to respect his privacy. One night, I asked, "What's with all the notebooks?"

"When we were separated, and the kids were in bed, or I felt alone, I would talk to God. It's a prayer journal, like the one you keep. I felt more connected to God when I wrote my feelings rather than prayed. I wrote praises and prayers for others too. The other notebook is notes, prayers, and poems for you. I would write to you when I had something on my mind but couldn't call and talk, or maybe it wasn't appropriate to tell you then. I thought one day we might want to remember these days."

"When do I get to read them?" I asked.

"One day," he said. "When you are ready."

"How will we know when I'm ready?"

"We will know."

I would soon learn that God was working on Clark while he was working on me. Coincidence? I think not. God was working and changing Clark's heart, and he used Clark as a vessel to intercede on my behalf.

Those notebooks were filled with prayers that Clark had been praying for me and my return home for months. He had also been praying for God to keep his heart pure.

I realized God had changed Clark in the same way he had changed me. We were completely different; the old had died, and new life was inside us.

God told me that he would bless my marriage if I was obedient to him and returned. I know because I argued with him and told him there was no way *that* marriage could be fixed. I sat there crying on my knees when he told me to go back. I was pleading with him. I didn't want to live the rest of my life in that marriage, but he said if I trusted him, he could make *that* marriage new. Nothing like before—better. I trusted him, and he did.

Things changed for both of us. We reconnected slowly, but it felt intimate and authentic.

During those many months of waiting, I thought, *Okay, God, hasn't it been long enough?* Obviously, it hadn't because even when we made progress and came out of that uneasy, uncomfortable part of my return home, we were still growing, learning, and being stretched by God.

During that time, I came to trust, forgive, and discover that love is more than an emotion or a feeling. Love is a decision and a promise; I decided to go back home with a promise to love Clark.

That obedience required me to sit in the uncomfortable and trust even when it involved waiting longer. Waiting longer required more prayer, more trust, and, ultimately, more personal growth, which led to change. Genuine, authentic growth from God would never have come if I had missed those middle, messy parts.

On many middle, messy days, I had to remind myself that God loves me unconditionally and beyond measure to calm my anxious heart. God is sovereign, he is faithful, and he is my Redeemer. I repeated those words until I felt my heart rate return to normal.

I gradually saw how Clark and I began seeking the Lord for our deficits and allowing him to pour into those instead of expecting the other person to do it.

By doing this, we rid each other of unnecessary expectations and became friends. The start of that friendship became the foundation on which our relationship would grow.

Sure, we were still learning and growing, but we had made so much progress. I was so proud of us, but it was more than just progress. The new life I saw in both of us couldn't be from ourselves; it could only have been delivered by Jesus because we were too selfish on our own.

It's funny because Clark was finally present with me. He was attentive to me, revealing parts of him I had never seen or known about. I loved it, but I didn't crave it the way I used to. I realized Jesus had filled those pieces of me that I thought were Clark's job to fill.

I was full already. It was such a refreshing, healing change! Clark is just an extra blessing here on earth to enjoy until I meet my ultimate true love. God didn't just redeem my marriage; he restored me.

*   *   *

Once you were alienated from God and were enemies in your minds because of your evil behavior. But now he has reconciled you by Christ's physical body through death to present you holy in his sight, without blemish and free from accusation—if you continue in your faith, established and firm, and do not move from the hope held out in the gospel.
—Colossians 1:21–23

CHAPTER 10

REDEMPTION

Remember the lies I internalized from my childhood? The ones that so terribly affected the first decade of my marriage?

As I shed those lies and replaced them with biblical truth, as I rested in God and stayed in communication with him, and as the Holy Spirit and I replaced those bandages regularly, I found healing.

As I found healing, my marriage found healing.

* * *

For he chose us in him before the creation of the world to be holy and
blameless in his sight. In love he predestined us for adoption to sonship
through Jesus Christ, in accordance with his pleasure and will.
—Ephesians 1:4–5

* * *

*The first lie wedged deep into my soul from childhood: I'm not wanted. I'm
inconvenient. I'm not good enough. I'm not important enough.*

That is the first feeling I remember ever being aware of, and the ache of it affected me to my core. This aching deep inside me was from the void of my soul crying out for God. It was a longing to be loved.

I replaced that with biblical truth: I'm wholly wanted. God made me because he wanted me. He has cared for me all my life because I'm not inconvenient to him. God has sought, wooed, and poured truth all over my life.

I think God is our most fundamental need. God is love, and love is the closest thing to God. As infants, we need love to thrive and grow, but as we develop, we must transition the view of love to God. Since God is love, as infants, we can't comprehend God, so I believe God gave us parents to love us developmentally and lead us to God.

Love is always supposed to lead you back to God. If you didn't grow up knowing or feeling loved, chances are you won't know God either. Since we are born with a void that was created for God to fill, but we don't know God, we look for other ways to fill that void. I certainly did, and I have a story full of heartache to prove it.

Genesis 1:1–2 says, "In the beginning, God created the heavens and the earth. Now the earth was formless and void." Why would God create a world that was formless and void? He was God. He had just created the universe out of nothing—why would it be formless and void?

After digging, studying, and asking many questions, I understood that the earth was like a desert. It isn't that the world wasn't good; it simply was not yet complete on purpose. God would later declare that all he made was "very good." Since the world needed to be formed in order, he created light, water, vegetation, and animals, and then he created us and gave us dominion over everything. Why did he create us last, and why did he give us dominion over everything he created before us?

God could have made a fully functioning world with a snap of his fingers; instead, he chose to start by creating an empty world and then adding to it, making it better. In other words, God made things better and shaped the empty world in such a way that it would benefit those who would soon inhabit it. God had us in mind all along when he created the world.

My interpretation of this is that God made the world good, but he left a void in it. To fill that void and make it whole, he created us. But when God created us, he created us empty and void as well, intending to fill the void in us. My conclusion is that we are created with the void on purpose. Just as we were the needed filling for the void in the world, God is the needed filling for the void in us. The Lord created the world to benefit us, and he created us to glorify him. Just as we made the world better with our presence, God makes us better when his presence takes up space in our hearts.

Why am I sharing all of this? I came to understand that my void, the hole in my heart, and the missing pieces of me that I longed for Clark to fill weren't intended to break or keep me broken; they were meant to complete me and heal me. My healing would not come from Clark; it would come from my Creator.

Since I didn't know that, I kept trying to fill that void with other things. When I understood that everyone was created with the same void, it meant that

I was not a defect or a reject. I was created on purpose—just like every one of you. The night I read the story about the woman at the well, the Holy Spirit convicted me that it was time to surrender, lay it all down, and let that aching void bring me back to God.

Surrender came first—and then came the guiding of the Holy Spirit. I poured myself into prayer, Bible study, quiet time, and worship. I started aligning my thoughts with truth, and that changed my behavior.

Surrender always has to come before sanctification.

When I started pursuing Jesus fully, I learned the truth about who he was versus what I believed about him based on my limited knowledge. Learning this truth showed me who I am in Christ. God showed me I was planned—so I couldn't be a mistake. If I'm not a mistake, then I am supposed to be here. I matter, and I'm wanted. I can take up as much space as I want without worrying about being "too much." I'm also not an inconvenience because I was made on purpose. In fact, I have been adopted into the kingdom of God. Just knowing I was wanted and accepted by God became enough for me.

Eventually, I came to the point where I fully believed that I was a child of God and that my identity came from Christ and not the world. If my identity came from God, I can't continue letting the world redefine what God has already defined.

* * *

Cast all your anxiety on him because he cares for you.
—1 Peter 5:7

* * *

The second big lie from my childhood: Self-reliance. I must care for myself without depending on anyone else.

I thought needing help meant you were weak and out of control, which made you vulnerable. Being vulnerable means you need to depend on other people. Vulnerability is weak, weak people are needy, and no one likes a needy person. Always have the upper hand and stay in control. Do it yourself. No one is going to help you anyway.

So I worked. I bought my own car and paid for my own insurance. And then, when I got married, I did everything around the house myself—everything with the kids. I made it so I needed Clark as little as possible.

Many times in my life, I would seek out God like a bloodhound, promising if he answered me, I would never leave him again—only to slowly quit seeking him, allowing my self-reliance to grow even stronger than before. In the earlier days of my marriage, I would pray for my marriage and see some change, but then I would forget about God and where that change came from. I'd quit praying until the next time it got so bad that I eventually stopped.

When I began replacing lies with truth, my dependence on God grew. As my dependence on God grew, my reliance on myself and the outside world began shrinking.

God made it clear that I depended more on myself than I did on him. I thought I was ultimately in control, and God was there as a backup when I couldn't figure it out.

When I understood that God wants us to rely on him just as much on good days as on bad ones, I started praying: "God, if my answers lead me away, I don't want them. I will trust you. I will wait on you. I want you. I want you more than a marriage. I want you more than I want answers."

God had to break me of my self-sufficiency. When I realized how much I depended on myself, it showed me how little I relied on God. The power of self-will is strong, and God's breaking process reveals both the power of our flesh and the power of God.

After I surrendered and God revealed my sinful self-reliance, I began praying for him to change me. I didn't just want to follow him out of obedience. I wanted a heart like his. I wanted a mind like his. I wanted to know his ways and walk with him.

Knowing God requires knowing ourselves. I began to understand that my "controlling feelings" were born out of survival mode from childhood. They wanted to protect and serve only me, but trusting God allowed him the opportunity to protect and serve where he saw was most beneficial to me, and it also gave him the greatest glory.

When God asked me to go home that night, I was pretty sure Clark would reject me, but I opened myself up to it and prayed: "Lord, just catch me when I fall." That took tremendous faith and vulnerability. I was asking God for help, and I didn't even realize it.

We are all going to fall, and we are all going to experience hurt, but we don't have to hide it, avoid it, or stuff it as I did. We have a God who wants to help us carry it, process it, change, and grow from it so that we can be changed people and help others.

I learned through that agonizing process that I was delaying God's promises every time I tried to take back control because all I was doing was getting in the way—and I wasn't fully relying on God to be God.

Clark used to say, "You'll figure it out or die trying before you ask for help."

I thought this was a compliment, but it wasn't. I wasted so many hours trying to figure things out instead of asking for help.

One day, Clark and I were in a tiff at my work. I don't remember what it was about, but I'm sure I was right (eye roll). The doctor walked in and sat down at the table with us. We got silent, not wanting to argue in front of him. He sat there silent for about sixty seconds, then said, "I love you, Kristie, but I do not know how Clark lives with the refusal of your vulnerability."

Whatever, I thought. *He's just a psychiatrist; what does he know?*

Clark said nothing even though I expected him to relish in delight that he had been validated. Instead, he pointed his finger in the air, signaling to God, and said, "Through him is the only way I know how to handle her."

That afternoon, I went to the doctor and asked, "Do I truly have a problem with vulnerability?" He nodded his head up and down so quickly I thought he would have head trauma. Okay, point received.

> We are all going to fall, and we are all going to experience hurt, but we don't have to hide it, avoid it, or stuff it like I did.

I knew about vulnerability. My therapist and I had been talking about it for quite some time. I knew it meant asking for help, taking chances, and trusting in faith that God will, in fact, catch you when you fall or give you wings to fly. I knew I had to start practicing this with Clark; it just felt so hard. It's like ripping off those bandages and revealing the yucky flesh that lives under there. Nobody wants to see that, but we can't grow or heal without those bandages being ripped off.

That meant vulnerability had to be practiced in my life. To practice vulnerability means to give up control. To give up control means relying on God. Relying on God means becoming vulnerable. Self-reliance and vulnerability can't co-exist.

God had to break me of my self-reliance to officiate this change inside of me. I had to surrender control to him and become vulnerable with Clark. Marriage is teamwork. That's why God took two and created one—so they could work together.

I had to understand that God puts people in our lives on purpose. We are called to be in community and intimacy. We must become vulnerable to become authentic.

* * *

For it is by grace you have been saved, through faith—and this is not from yourselves, it is the gift of God—not by works, so that no one can boast.
— Ephesians 2:8–9

*   *   *

The third great lie of my childhood; Love must be earned.

I thought I had to please everyone to be loved or cared for: my stepmom, my dad, and then Clark. Be better, do things differently. I was trying to take control of the situation with my own rules and expectations to get what I wanted: the love I needed. It was exhausting, and it didn't even work.

Learning my identity in Christ and believing that my Creator accepts me was game-changing. It helped put all the other lies into perspective. Love is not earned. Love is not transactional between us flawed people; the only transaction ever made in love was made when Jesus went to the cross, and because of that, we don't ever have to earn it. It's ours if we accept it.

Since love doesn't have to be earned, this freed my mind from constantly trying to please people. I could quit trying to be who I thought I needed to be for everyone else, focus on who God created me to be, and be that person no matter who I'm around. I could quit trying to earn love and accept myself as the flawed woman God created and loves.

In the middle of learning all of this, when Clark came home one day, the house was a mess. I had not felt well that day and had taken a nap. When I woke up, the place looked like a frat house, and I didn't have the energy or the time to get it in order or make dinner before he got home.

I knew Clark hated messiness and chaos, and I sprang into action, despite feeling horrible. Then I was suddenly reminded that Clark and I had decided to love each other unconditionally when we got back together—not just when things were good—and everything was going well. I had a bad day, and I didn't have to pay for it because love is not earned.

I braced myself for when Clark got home. I was ready to go into defense mode, but that didn't feel right anymore. Instead, I prayed: "Lord, please show me how to handle this, guide my emotions, open my heart, and cover my mouth." I thought, *If Clark loves me unconditionally as he says, let's see what happens when that's put to the test.*

When Clark walked in, I could see in his eyes that he was shocked, but all he said was, "Did a party go on here today without me?"

I held my breath. Surely that wasn't all. I gave him an exhausted look; it was like he had gotten it. All of a sudden, it clicked in him.

He called all the kids down and said, "Let's clean up this mess while mom takes a bath and see if we can find dinner."

I cried in the bathtub that night. I could not believe what had just occurred.

Just because something bad happens, I don't behave as I should, or I have a terrible day doesn't mean Clark stops loving me. And I had to remember the same was true for him and do the same if I wanted him to extend that grace to me.

One night, Clark came home frustrated and didn't want to talk, which was weird because we had been doing so well at that. Immediately, I thought, *What did I do wrong?*

I got worked up inside, my heart was racing, and I kept asking him what was wrong.

He kept saying nothing.

That would have been the point where I picked a fight to take control of the situation. That night, I walked away from the situation and prayed: "Lord, I don't know what I did or if I even did anything, but if I did, will you help me make it right and use it to grow us closer and calm my heart?"

When the kids went to bed, Clark told me he had seen a horrible wreck happen on his way home. That night, I learned not to take everything personally. Not every one of Clark's emotions was about me, and I didn't have to worry that it was my fault if he was upset—and immediately believe he would stop loving me.

A peace flooded my heart and took me back to the day when I first felt God's love was enough. Oh, how it filled me! I had finally come to a place of peacefulness where I felt loved, which baffled me.

How could I feel loved when there was no one to love me? It was because of the presence of the Lord living in my heart. God loved me. I knew it—and I felt it.

I finally realized that Clark wasn't responsible for making me feel loved, valued, or worthy, and it wasn't my job to do the same for him.

Neither of us had to earn love—from God or from each other. It was a game-changing revelation.

* * *

Are not five sparrows sold for two pennies? Yet not one of them is forgotten by God. Indeed, the very hairs of your head are all numbered. Don't be afraid; you are worth more than many sparrows.

—Luke 12:6–7

* * *

The fourth lie was: I am not worthy of sacrifice.

Not feeling worthy or important kept me from asking for the things I needed or wanted. I was so used to the answer "no" that I just quit asking. If you don't ask, they can't say no; if they don't say no, then you aren't being reminded you aren't worthy or important.

I would not ask my parents for the simplest of things—even if they were a necessity. I wouldn't ask Clark to babysit or even watch the kids so I could take a bath alone. Living that way kept me in bondage to the enemy's lies.

I finally replaced that lie with the truth: I am worthy simply because God made me and loves me. This affected my daily life and decisions.

For example, a weekend women's retreat was coming up at our church. I casually mentioned that I thought it would be fun and could be a good way to meet new people.

Clark said, "I think you should go."

I said, "But it's for the whole weekend."

"So?" he said.

"Clark, Carter is only two. You can't watch him and the girls all weekend."

"Why not?"

"That would be too much on you."

"Kristie, do you want to go?"

"Yes. No. Maybe. Kinda."

I was nervous and scared for several reasons. I didn't want him to have so much responsibility while I was away "playing," and I had never done anything like that. I didn't have friends who went away and were their own person outside of being a mom and a wife. But those were the things my therapist told me were essential to growing into myself and becoming more than just a mom and a wife.

I blurted out, "Yes, I want to go."

"Okay then. Sign up and let me worry about the rest."

It was the first time I had ever asked to go away and do something on my own. It was the first time I had ever expressed a request to Clark that I knew would require some sacrifice on his part. He rose to the occasion without hesitation and did well.

Practicing things like that over time gave me a voice. There were times when Clark said no, and at first, that intimidated me, but over time, these things were essential for me growing into myself and figuring out that I was worthy of more.

When I realized I was worthy of more, I understood that I was also worthy of sacrifice. It was okay to inconvenience someone on my behalf because isn't that what love is? Sacrificing yourself for the benefit of another? If I am loved, I am worthy of sacrifice, which makes me enough.

Knowing I was worthy brought life into my soul. Knowing I was valued as Kristie and not just defined as a mom or a wife opened up new opportunities and possibilities for what I could do and who I could become. It gave me the confidence to step outside my safety net and find hobbies and activities I enjoyed—even at the risk of failure.

God was refining me and stripping away the hardwired toxic traits and lies in me. He showed me how to think more like him and less like me.

*   *   *

For, "Who has known the mind of the Lord so as to
instruct him?" But we have the mind of Christ.
—1 Corinthians 2:16

*   *   *

This was the lie: I have no self-agency. I am incapable of making my own decisions.

When I entered into a right relationship with God with a pure heart, seeking to know and do his will over mine, I found myself pursuing him. I found myself clinging to him—and not just in my times of brokenness. I learned about the strength that I can have only through him.

I'm not in control, and I do not need to be controlled.

Through scripture, my therapist, and time, God helped me replace this lie with truth: I am a grown woman who is fully capable of taking care of myself because God takes care of me and gives me all I need.

Mostly, it was during that separation period when I learned I was more than capable of making my own decisions:

- I made the decision to leave Clark—without any assurances that things would end well.
- I made all the decisions for my own life when we were separated: finances, time management, relationships, everything. And not only did I do fine—I did *well*.
- I made the decision to follow God's leading in returning. No one made me do that. God told me to, but he would never have forced me. He led and gave me strength, and *I* did it.

More than decision-making, my self-agency increased when I ceased taking responsibility for Clark's behavior—or anyone else's—and took responsibility only for mine. When I realized I was the only one I could control, my life got a lot cleaner, more straightforward, and free.

* * *

When we don't see progress, we can think God isn't working. Oh, but he is still working. He can change our situation in a heartbeat. We simply aren't aware until it's time for his purpose to be revealed—at a time when he knows we are ready.

When he changes us, we are different. I am not the girl I was seventeen years ago when all this started. In fact, I'm not the same woman today as I was three years ago when I started writing this book—and thank God for that!

True faith in God changes everything. It changes the way you think, act, and speak.

God did resurrect my marriage, just like he promised me he would. Clark and I have been set free from the bondage we once lived in. Of course, we have some scars from those days; they were pretty rough. I used to be ashamed of those scars. Those scars told my dirtiest secrets or reverted me back to my older version—like the scrapbook did—but now I understand that through those scars, I can give my greatest testimony about a man who set me free. That man redeemed my marriage and restored my soul.

For years, I didn't tell anyone about our story. People would hear me talk about the present day and ask, "What's the secret?"

I would only say, "Jesus is the secret." That always left me feeling yucky.

Jesus truly is the secret, but I felt like I was deceiving them a little because I didn't want to tell our dark secret of how we almost got a divorce or how toxic we were to each other at one time. I feared they might think differently of us; we weren't those people anymore.

I didn't like talking about those days because they were hard, and if we aren't those people anymore, why keep revisiting them? One day, I shared my story with a struggling friend, and she looked at me with tears in her eyes and said the one thing I never thought was possible. She said, "Your story gives me hope for my marriage. If y'all can survive that, surely we can too."

You see, I had never thought about my most painful times as anything that could give anyone hope. But the more I opened up to others about my story, the more vulnerable they became with me. I learned there is so much heartache out there that stems from brokenness and infidelity, but we are all too ashamed to talk about it. We want to hush it up and don't want anyone to know. We try to sweep it under the rug and hope we can heal ourselves. After all, isn't that what I tried to do?

Well, I won't stay quiet anymore. Jesus told me to take my scars, show them to the brokenhearted, and point them toward the one true healer. He can redeem their marriages and restore their hearts. If the sins of my past and my darkest days can lead someone to Jesus, I don't care what the rest of the world thinks.

I want to stand up and yell, "Yes, my life was a mess! My childhood was broken, dysfunctional, and traumatic, and Jesus restored my soul."

I want to say, "My marriage was dead, ugly, and it dishonored God ... but guess what? It doesn't anymore. It may have been dead, but it is resurrected. Glory be to God!"

Jesus healed us, and he wants to do the same for you.

I walk a little differently now. I'm not scared to show my brokenness. I'm not afraid to tell my story. The person I used to be and the marriage I used to have doesn't have any power over me anymore. The only power I will allow it to have is the power to tell of God's mercy and grace. I don't want to forget that. I don't want to pretend it didn't happen for the sake of what others might think. I'm not scared or ashamed. God has truly set me free.

The night I wrestled with God and went home out of obedience changed my life and the trajectory of my life. My kids benefited from it. They had the privilege of growing up in a home with both parents present. I am so glad because I don't think I could have made it through those teenage years without Clark by my side.

Clark became my helpmate, my partner, and my best friend. He is my absolute favorite person on this earth. God allowed my marriage to survive, and he allowed it to thrive—just like he promised.

It didn't happen overnight, but Clark went from zero in my book to hero. Clark allowed Jesus to transform his life, and I think Jesus outdid himself with that transformation because he is the best man I know.

Let me be clear. Clark and I do not have a perfect marriage. There are still "discussions" that are unpleasant and days when both of us think, *Who is this person?* We have seasons that are just plain work. We're still two flawed people, and on this side of heaven, we always will be.

One more thing to be very clear about: Redemption and healing didn't come to our marriage until Clark and I both, individually, came close to Jesus. It was personal and individual before it was the two of us.

* * *

I am my beloved's and my beloved is mine.
—Song of Songs 6:3

* * *

I would never have thought it possible that Clark and I would make it past ten years—much less twenty-seven—and that our marriage could be the refuge and blessing that it is. "But God." Those two words make all the difference, giving us peace, courage, and hope. Now we know that "but God" can do all things. I don't say this to brag about how great we are. I say this because I want you to see—and I hope you have seen—how broken we were and how far we have come with the healing power of Jesus Christ as our guide in the past seventeen years.

The redemption of our marriage improved our life, and it created a new life. I got pregnant a year after I came home. I had my tubes tied after my third pregnancy and was told no babies would ever come from my body again. The tubes were tied, cut, and removed.

But Jesus! Isn't that a sentence all on its own? But Jesus. I like to think that Carter was a gift to us, just like God sent Noah a rainbow for his obedience. To me, Carter was the reassurance that we were finally doing it right this time--God's way.

Six years ago, God brought another child into our lives through adoption. We weren't actively seeking to adopt; honestly, we were trying to make it through three teenagers. We were in the thick of a challenging season with them when this little angel showed up. Neither of us had thought about another baby, but we knew well enough that if God brought us to it, he would get us through it. We had no idea how painful the process would be—But God.

Four years ago, we finally finished remodeling the last room in our house (the house that almost broke us), and we were so proud of it. We stood there admiring the bathroom; it looked like something out of a magazine. I giggled and said, "Told ya it would take ten years to finish this house."

Clark gave me a fist bump and said, "We did it together, babe."

"Can we finally enjoy it now?"

"I think so." He came over and hugged me.

It was indeed a celebration. I loved him and this life we had fought so hard for, and I was ready to enjoy it all. Truly absorb it all.

But God.

God asked us to sell that house two weeks later. Two weeks! I only had the bathtub of my dreams for two weeks, and God asked me to give it up. Of course, by then, I had learned that if God says move, you don't stay a minute longer.

We put our house on the market a month later, and it sold immediately. We sold our home and three-fourths of our belongings. We had no idea what God's plans were beyond that; we had no further instructions. Everyone told us we were foolish, but Clark and I were okay with taking risks as long as we knew the Lord was leading. We were confident that God would guide our steps and direct our path, and we waited for further instructions, believing God only wanted the best for us.

Six months later, God led us two hours away from Columbia to a town called Campobello. We giggled because we didn't know Campobello existed, but we left everything familiar and safe, including all our friends and family, in faith that God was ready to use us differently.

As God knows best, Campobello was precisely where we needed to be for this next season of life. This season would teach us many lessons and grow us closer to the Lord and each other. In this season, this book would be birthed—and God would again ask us to leave security behind and follow him.

Never underestimate the power of a decision that is made in obedience.

*   *   *

Therefore if you have any encouragement from being united with Christ, if any comfort from his love, if any common sharing in the Spirit, if any tenderness and compassion, then make my joy complete by being like-minded, having the same love, being one in spirit and of one mind. Do nothing out of selfish ambition or vain conceit. Rather, in humility value others above yourselves, not looking to your own interests but each of you to the interests of the others.
—Philippians 2:1–4

CHAPTER 11

FOR YOU

I believed the lies from childhood and adolescence and brought them into my marriage. The result was a decade of emotional pain and loss in my marriage and life in general.

I didn't have peace, and I didn't have internal or external contentment. I did not have a marriage that honored God, and I didn't get to experience the ongoing personal transformation that a follower of Jesus should experience.

Because I've felt broken and incomplete my whole life, I went into my marriage with Clark looking for it to make me whole and complete. I thought it would be the one thing that could make me whole.

It didn't happen that way. No matter how much he did, I still never felt loved by him. Not feeling loved by him made me feel even worse about myself. *Why doesn't he love me naturally? We are married! This is his job, right?*

Since he didn't love me correctly, the way I needed—the way that filled my void, my hole, and the emptiness in my soul—the only thing I knew how to do was try harder. Be better and do things differently.

I wasn't thinking about what Clark needed or wanted outside of myself because I believed what he needed and wanted was the same thing I did, a marriage filled with love, which would bring happiness. He didn't seem like he was trying very hard to get to the same destination I was, and it caused a lot of pain and trouble for more than a decade of marriage.

I continuously told Clark what he was doing wrong and how to fix it, but he didn't seem to understand or care because he never got it right. Exhausted and unsatisfied, I grew tired of chasing after his love and unknowingly tried to replace it with the kids, a new house, friends, and things, which always left me unhappy or fulfilled.

Still, whether I acknowledged it or not, the hole was always there. The pain somehow always found its way back to me. I thought the right person or thing could fill my hole—the void in my heart where something was missing—and I would finally be complete.

I entered this marriage believing it would give me a sense of worth and identity. After all, isn't that what idols do? I had no idea Clark had become my idol.

One big problem with worshipping idols is it robs you. How could our home be a place of peace or contentment when neither of us knew what it meant to rest in our full acceptance and love from God?

Clark and I tried so hard at various points in that first decade. We both put in the work, and that's just what it was: work. It felt so hard. Like a checklist. Nothing was easy and light about us. I didn't have a good example of a good marriage, and I thought, *Maybe this is what a normal marriage feels like.* If I didn't want normal, I would need to try harder—so I did.

The problem with trying harder and harder to fix things yourself is that it doesn't work. You also get completely exhausted and miss out on the rest and reassurance that comes from God.

In the first years, we argued heatedly. Then, we went through a season where we didn't argue, which was only because we ignored all the problems. We just cohabitated together peacefully, totally ignoring the massive gap between us. Clark worked and paid all the bills, ensuring that we had the things we wanted and needed. I took care of the kids alone. There were hurt feelings, but we didn't talk about them. We didn't talk about anything of substance.

I believed the lie that told me I would never be good enough. No matter what I did, it would never be enough. When God said he loved everybody, I didn't think he really meant me. I thought I would be alone forever. I thought no one would ever love me. I thought I wasn't a good mom, and I thought I was messing up everything.

I lost so much through believing and living the lies of the enemy:

- Good moms don't need breaks or leave their kids.
- Let husbands do whatever they want as long as they provide. Providing is their only job.
- Clark was doing his job—so why should I ask for or expect more? He loves me by working.

I didn't know these were lies because they were the truth I was raised by. What did I witness growing up? When dad wasn't happy, then it was up to us to make him happy. When we didn't, it was our fault. We must be doing it wrong.

This lie led me to believe Clark was responsible for my happiness, but he isn't. Only God can fill me with truth, acceptance, love, and assurance.

Learning this took me a long time, but it changed my life.

* * *

What God used to transform me: His Word

> Your word is a lamp for my feet, a light on my path.
> —Psalm 119:105

* * *

Coming out from under those lies, learning, accepting, and internalizing the truth, and adapting my behaviors in accordance with truth took time, and it is an ongoing process.

God used several elements to transform me. First, he used his Word. Friends, if you want to know what God thinks about you, read scripture. God's love, acceptance, forgiveness, and guidance are all over the place. I can't overemphasize how powerful the Word of God was in changing me from the inside out.

Learning God and his Word have taught me truth and delivered freedom. God's Word assures me that God loves me because he created me. I don't have to earn his love or be good enough. He loves me simply because he is love.

I had to memorize God's Word, his truth, his love, and his promises and repeat them to myself when I felt the enemy attacking. God's Word clearly states that the enemy comes only to kill, steal, and destroy, and he is the only one who delivers shame, regret, rejection, and fear. When I started to think in such a way, I immediately prayed for the Lord to speak truth over me. This helped me begin identifying the truth over the lies.

I began to be able to identify the enemy's attacks more quickly, and I could replace his lies with God's truth.

I had to take every thought captive.

God would say, "Do you remember my promises?"

"Yes," I would respond.

"What were they?"

"You will restore my marriage and make it even better than it was before."

"Then remain in me, and I will remain in you."

I had to let God's words refill me daily and even hourly. Though it took a long time, I had to cling to his promise to restore my marriage.

When thoughts would come into my head and tell me I would be alone forever because no one would ever love me, I immediately knew that was the enemy because he is the only one who wants to bring shame, rejection, and fear. Jesus came to bring hope, light, forgiveness, and salvation. If our thoughts point toward anything other than that, that's the enemy.

If the voice I hear does not offer hope, encouragement, love, or truth, it is a lie. It is not from God—and we don't listen to lies or give them any power to hold space in our heads. The only way to defeat lies is with the truth.

When the enemy tries to tell me I'm not good enough, I tell him I am more valuable than gold.

When he tells me I'm messing up my kids, I pray for guidance.

When he tells me I will never be loved, I tell him I am adopted into God's chosen family—so I *am* loved.

When he says I will never be forgiven, I remind him that I have been redeemed and set free.

When he tells me I'm not beautiful, I remind him that I am my creator's masterpiece.

* * *

Therapy

A therapist is just a person, imperfect, but all the same, I wouldn't be where I am today without the godly therapists God put in my life. We need a community and skilled people who can help us see who we are, where we need healing, and how to pursue it.

My therapists provided a safe place for me to process—sometimes vent—and calm, steady, objective insight. They opened my eyes to the truth of my childhood traumas. They helped me see the importance of dealing with that trauma head-on, wholeheartedly, and at a pace set by the Holy Spirit.

They opened my eyes to my own faults and helped me take responsibility for myself—without taking responsibility for Clark or my parents. And they were so encouraging when I needed to cry, felt confused, or was afraid. They were, truly, God's gift to me for my own healing and growth.

* * *

Time

Time doesn't heal all wounds—only Jesus can do that—but he doesn't do it in a hurry. Remember my nurse friend who told me about how they change bandages so often on burn victims? So their healing is complete and not partial? That takes time, and there's no substitute for it.

God used the passage of time to heal me, grow me, and redeem my marriage. Time wouldn't do it by itself, but as God worked in me and I did my part, over time, I changed.

And Clark did too.

* * *

You were taught, with regard to your former way of life, to put off your old self, which is being corrupted by its deceitful desires; to be made new in the attitude of your minds; and to put on the new self, created to be like God in true righteousness and holiness.
—Ephesians 4:22–24

* * *

What I gained in my transformation: Marriage Redeemed

If you had told me on my tenth anniversary that I would be in a redeemed marriage, I would have told you that sounded nice, but you were dreaming. Yet here we are—in exactly that. It's not as good as the young love days of high school; it is better. God has changed Clark in the same way he has changed me. We are both completely different people. The old has died, and there is new life inside of us.

The new life in our marriage isn't something we white-knuckled or some magical thing; it could only have been delivered from Jesus, and that gives me hope and faith that God still isn't done with us. He still has more in store for us. I know it.

* * *

A True Sense of Self

I know who I am now. I know how loved and accepted I am. I know my value and my worth.

I also know who I'm not. I'm not a victim, unable to make my own decisions, subject to the whims and demands and opinions of others. Like the apostle Paul, I don't worry about being compared to others. I just want to make sure I fit God's plan. We shouldn't let other people's evaluations of personality, gifts, or service be overplayed in our lives. Our gifts, callings, and personal boundaries are set by God alone. A healthy spiritual self-image gives me the freedom to work for Christ.

* * *

Healing from Childhood

Thanks to God's Word, my therapists, and a lot of hard internal work, I have been blessed with a lot of healing from my childhood.

Looking back, I can see that both of my parents were broken people from broken childhoods. They were doing the best they could or what they had been taught or exposed to. Of course, I didn't know that then. I needed years of therapy to see that. Knowing that doesn't erase the scars that were inflicted upon me, or take away the pain, but it does give me some grace for them now.

Just as importantly, I don't have to pass on my own childhood hurts to Clark, my girls, or my grandchildren.

* * *

You can experience the same thing. The first step, I believe, is believing and internalizing what scripture says about your identity in Christ. Here is a partial list:

- Therefore, if anyone is in Christ, the new creation has come: The old has gone, the new is here! (2 Corinthians 5:17)
- But you are a chosen people, a royal priesthood, a holy nation, God's special possession, that you may declare the praises of him who called you out of the darkness into his wonderful light. (1 Peter 2:9)
- Before I formed you in the womb I knew you, before you were born I set you apart; I appointed you as a prophet to the nations. (Jeremiah 1:5)
- I have been crucified with Christ and I no longer live, but Christ lives in me. The life I now live in the body, I live by faith in the Son of God, who loved me and gave himself for me. (Galatians 2:20)
- For we are God's handiwork, created in Christ Jesus to do good works, which God prepared in advance for us to do. (Ephesians 2:10)
- Don't you not know that your bodies are temples of the Holy Spirit, who is in you, whom you have received from God? You are not your own; you were bought at a price. Therefore honor God with your bodies. (1 Corinthians 6:19–20)
- And to put on the new self, created to be like God in true righteousness and holiness. (Ephesians 4:24)

You have to stockpile God's truth in your mind and in your heart.

True healing allows us to find our identities in Christ and not in the world. Our identities lead us to our purposes. God wants all his children to know and experience this, but he does it only in partnership with us. God won't force anything, and he won't wave any magic wands. He will do amazing things, but we must be willing and active participants.

*   *   *

Secondly, you need to do the hard work of dealing with your past, especially if there was any trauma.

This entire book has been the story of how the lies and trauma of my childhood followed me into marriage and adult life and how I had to face those things and deal with them to heal and grow. I could only do that with God's help and strength, but I still had to do it.

We can't heal from what we don't acknowledge. This is especially true in trauma cases. The first step in healing trauma is acknowledging its existence. You have to come to terms with the fact that what you experienced wasn't normal. When you dismiss or excuse your trauma as simply a regular part of life, you deny its impact on you.

Whatever the hurt is, it steals something from us, and without God, we are left wondering how to replace it. I know I did. I thought Clark was my remedy, but all that did was create another hurt and void, which led me to cover up or ignore that I was hurting.

Digging in my heels and declaring that I wanted a real change from above allowed God to transform me into what he had purposed, and that is something only he can do. I had to choose: Did I want God's promises and blessings—or did I want easy? The same is true for you.

Starting from scratch is easy work; anyone can keep running, start over, and build new. That's all self-made stuff—and that's exactly what I tried to do in the beginning. Why? Because it's easier. It might be easier, but it isn't healthier!

Staying broken is easy. Healing is the hard part, but you can do hard things.

Our past experiences have made us who we are today, but we don't have to remain those people. All around the world, God is redeeming what seems irredeemable:

> "He who was seated on the throne," said, "Behold,
> I am making all things new."
> —Revelation 21:5

God did not say he was making *all new things;* he said he is making *all things new.* Think about that for a minute. God's innate reaction to brokenness is restoration.

* * *

Third, you have to do the hard work of breaking harmful behavioral patterns.

The most harmful pattern I needed God to help me break was my idolatry. I idolized Clark. I longed for love, and since Clark was the only one who had given it to me, I thought he was the only one who ever could. I believed I'd never be loved again if he didn't love me anymore.

An idol is whatever you pick up to fill the hole or the void. It fills something inside of you that you're longing for or lacking. Idols don't have to be bad things; an idol is anything that separates you from God.

I know firsthand that we don't understand the severity of this hole, this void, and we ignore it and attempt to fix it with other things besides God. Isn't that exactly what I did? I had to break that habit and put God entirely on the throne of all my life and heart, which I still have to do daily. It's an ongoing process and will be the same for you.

It's easier to break free from harmful behavior patterns if you can create a healthy habit to replace it with. That will look different for everyone.

* * *

A fourth harmful pattern you might need to break is no longer assuming responsibility for others.

I had to recognize that I am the only person I'm responsible for. I can only change myself—not anyone else.

By the same token, I had to recognize that no one else was responsible for filling my emptiness. Only God could do that.

When I realized Clark wasn't responsible for making me feel loved, valued, or worthy, I understood it wasn't my job to do the same for him. This was a significant breakthrough.

I also had to change my attitude and my mindset. That became easier after learning the truth and living it, but some days—most days—I still have to take every thought captive.

* * *

Last, you have to break the harmful pattern of ignoring or covering the hurt.

In the first decade of our marriage, I often did those things when I was hurting. I got busier to cover the hurt. If I leave Clark alone, maybe the hurt will go away. Don't talk about hard things. Did that work? No. It only added layers of hurt over my wounds. I had to change that.

Now, we talk. We check in. We go on dates. We're honest and open with each other. There is no more hiding, covering, or ignoring. It's so much better this way.

Learning to voice your hurt and pain will likely require vulnerability, but life is much better this way. Vulnerability breaks barriers and allows authentic relationships to take root. Nothing is more refreshing on this side of heaven than knowing that someone knows things about your precious, flawed self and loves you in spite of it. It's a beautiful feeling.

When we finally expose and heal ourselves, it allows us to help others. It takes a village, y'all!

* * *

My sweet, sweet friend, if you've made it this far with me, know that it is no accident because I have been praying over this book for two years that it will find its way into your very hands. The point of putting this story together is this: I want you to know that, no matter where you are, what you have done, or what has been done to you, as long as you are still breathing, God's plan is to redeem and restore you. And he will! God is able to free you from anything that is holding you back. He wants to come alongside you and carry your hurt, your pain, and your burdens. He loves you that much.

If you are hurting and want to start healing—or if you are trying to heal, but can't find healing—don't give up! Listen to me right now. You are not alone! Jesus is always with you, and if I were beside you right now, I would hug you and remind you that you are so much stronger than you think. I would tell you that you were created on purpose, with a purpose, and for a purpose.

I believe with my whole heart that God is waiting on you. He wants you to experience healing in your life and be set free. Turn to him, internalize your identity according to his Word, and do whatever hard work is needed to walk in his truth. And I pinkie-promise you and solemnly swear to you that he will give you grace, courage, strength, and healing. I can't promise things will be rosy. In fact, I can just about promise that walking with God will be hard sometimes. But God. You will never be alone.

And in the end, his truth will set you free. I don't know what that will look like for you personally or in any relationship in your life, but if you set aside your idols and turn to Jesus, he will heal your heart.

Printed in the United States
by Baker & Taylor Publisher Services